ADAPTATION

MY LIFE IN MONTANA

WITH KIDS, PETS

AND

A COUNTRY VET

A

MEMOIR

BY

GEORGIA L. ALDERINK

Copyright © 2014 Georgia L. Alderink

ISBN: 1494276216
ISBN-13: 978-1494276218

All rights reserved

including the right of reproduction

in whole or in part or in any form

A License Agreement granting use of Copyrighted Artwork of 5 cartoons by Dr. Robert M. Miller, aka RMM, aka Bob Miller, was signed on February 7, 2013.

All photographs are from the Alderink family collection.

Self-published by Georgia L. Alderink and printed by CreateSpace, an Amazon.com company

For my daughters, Jill and Kay
and
for memories of Sue and Joel.

THANKS TO A FEW FRIENDS

To my writing group, Cheryl Davis, Kimberly Mitchell, Kari Harms and Trey Ferguson, who told me, "You need to explain this better."

To Earnie Montgomery, whose advice was, "Add more description."

And thanks also to my husband, Fred, who, whenever I complained, said, "Of course you can do it," and patiently continued to correct errors in the veterinary stories and proofread the entire manuscript.

PROLOGUE

Like a playful child, this memoir does not go from Point A straight to Point B. It consists of accounts, essays, stories, and letters, which twist and turn and double back on themselves.

The memoir begins when Fred and I married and moved to Montana, and continues with us simultaneously raising kids and practicing veterinary medicine. The main emphasis is on life with our children, though, in retrospect, the years they lived with us were few.

My comment about writing a memoir has been, "Whose life is so interesting that others want to read about it?" But I like to write and thought if I wrote mostly about our kids, they, at least, might find it interesting.

No one can write down memories without changing reality in some way. These incidents are simply as I remember them.

So here you are, Jill and Kay. You can say, "That wasn't how it was. I distinctly remember it differently." And your memories will be correct to you, just as mine are to me.

GAMBLING ON MONTANA

Fred and I set our marriage date: Monday, August 15, 1960. The place: Roseau, Minnesota. The time: 10:30 a.m. We quit our jobs, mine with Midwest Planning and Research in Minneapolis, Minnesota, and Fred's with Dr. Sook, the veterinarian in Marshall. After the wedding we planned to sally forth in Fred's jaunty 1957 yellow and white Fairlane Ford and head west–a part honeymoon, part business trip. Our hope was to find the perfect spot to start a veterinary practice, preferably in Montana.

"How do you like camping?" Fred asked, shortly before our marriage.

"I've never been camping." Even I heard the trepidation in my voice.

Camping? Marriage meant changes, that's understandable. But I'd be leaving my apartment, my job, the city I enjoyed, my state, my family, and even my identity. Instead of answering to Georgie Brateng, my name for 19 years, I would have to get used to hearing either Georgia or Mrs. Fred Alderink.

Yes, I admonished myself, as I kicked the gravel in the drive thoughtfully. There's lots you're going to have to learn, and part of that might be how to get rid of your cowardly streak. Images of bears, big cats, snakes, spiders, and a long list of possible calamities ran through my brain, but I said thoughtfully. "No, I've never been camping. It might be an interesting adventure."

Fred had only worked for a year after he graduated from veterinary school, so he couldn't have stashed away too much money, of that I felt reasonably sure, and I certainly knew I hadn't set aside anything in my two years in the work force. In fact, Fred paid a couple of my bills just before we left Minneapolis to go up to Roseau.

Camping was cheap and Fred liked it. Also, I suspected he fancied the idea of his bride being willing to camp on her honeymoon. I bought a couple of white suitcases, not at all suitable for camping, and a pair of jeans; the sum total of my preparations.

My soon-to-be husband gathered his camping equipment: an army issue pup tent, two army issue sleeping bags, and a battered, green Coleman camp stove. He also owned a set of aluminum cookware, each piece nestled cleverly together, and a large cooler. Years later, when we camped in Grand Canyon National Park, a young couple next to us pulled out the makings for an entire gourmet meal (some dish with asparagus and mushrooms) and proceeded to cook, sending up a mist of delicious aromas. They ended their meal with wine in wine glasses.

On this camping/honeymoon/business trip I did well to learn how to fry hamburgers and pork chops on either an open fire or on the camp stove. Meals consisted of boiled or fried potatoes, a canned vegetable of some kind, either canned or fresh fruit, and fried meat. Our appetites were good, our digestive systems young; we survived quite well.

Not every night was spent camping. Occasionally the Ford made stops at motels, or at the homes of friends Fred had made on his western treks during college; the trips which were the impetus for his dream of a Montana vet practice. However, we camped a good share of the time, sometimes in campgrounds, sometimes not, sometimes in the old army pup tent, sometimes just out under the stars.

***

My learning experiences did not stop with campfire cooking and sleeping under the stars. Fred had packed only a few dress shirts, which he used for Sunday meetings and occasionally when meeting some local dignitary. Laundromats abounded, and I knew how to use a washing machine. But, even had laundromats supplied their clients with irons and ironing boards, one problem remained; I had no idea how to iron a man's white dress shirt. "How can I get these shirts ironed?" I asked Fred.

"We'll find a laundry/dry cleaning place and hire them done."

I'm not sure we could find such a place now. Laundry/dry cleaning establishments with which I am acquainted, take your laundry, give you a slip, a future pick-up date, and send it all off to some obscure place. Somehow you get your own clothes back. But, as we cruised through a small North Dakota town on Highway 2, we spied a sign, "Laundry/Dry Cleaning" in large print and under that, "All Work Done on Premises."

Clutching two white shirts under my arm, I opened the glass door. The moist, clean, soapy smell transported me back to Mom's basement on laundry day, and I stood, poised to step inside, but listening in my head to the old Maytag thumping like a beating heart on every Monday morning. Was that a whiff of homesickness?

An older, Italian man, a white tee shirt pulled over his round tummy, shook out a red handkerchief and wiped his brown, sweaty forehead before he looked up.

"Come in," he greeted me. "You have shirts?" He showed off a gold tooth in a wide smile. "Need washing? Ironing?"

"Ironing."

He scrutinized me carefully and apparently sensed this young bride did not know the first thing about ironing a man's shirt.

"You come back here Girlie," he said, lifting up the hinged part of the counter. "I show proper way."

He laid the collar of the shirt on the board, backside up, smoothing it with his fingers. "Start collar like this," he instructed, and went through the whole procedure; back and front of the collar, shoulders, cuffs, sleeves, ending with the body of the shirt. He whistled between his teeth as he worked, making a symphony with the hissing steam.

When ironed to his satisfaction he said, "Now I show to fold. First, button buttons, then turn face down."

Again he whistled through every step; folding one fourth of the shirt straight down from the shoulder, laying the sleeve down neatly, making sure the cuffs were tidy, then doing the same with the other side of the shirt. Last, he folded one third of the shirt up and the top down. Finished with both shirts, he patted them and smiled at me. "There you go, Girlie."

With every shirt I've ironed since, I've followed his instructions. Often I think of my instructor in the art of ironing and folding shirts and wonder if I've ever done anything so helpful or said something so kind that it is remembered 50 years later.

***

Everywhere we went Fred searched out the county extension offices and requested statistics about cattle populations and weather. In the process of conversing with these local people, he'd also come away with a feel for the community. We always stopped to visit the veterinarian who served whatever area we were in. I don't remember all the places we checked. Fairview, Montana, just over the North Dakota line, I do remember. Fred didn't think much of Fairview.

"Why don't you like Fairview?" I asked. "They even offered to build us a clinic."

"Oh, I don't know. I don't like to feel indebted to anyone."

"But we'd pay rent. We wouldn't be in their debt."

"Fairview is barely over the North Dakota line. That's pretty close to relatives."

I didn't point out to him the entire length of North Dakota stretched between Fairview, Montana and Roseau, Minnesota. He didn't want Fairview, so I kept quiet.

Cutbank's population actively sought a vet. The day we pulled into town, wind blew the U.S. flag at the post office straight out. "Just a little breeze," everyone said. Little breeze? More like a land based hurricane! On we went to Western Montana.

***

Late one afternoon, close to Troy, we drove into a camping area to spend the night. A gurgling creek of clear, blue-green water meandered through the campsites, but when we drove slowly by the sites, we saw no potable water faucet and no privy. It was not an improved campground. My heart sank. Toilets and showers took precedence over beauty as far as I was concerned.

By the time we finished our pork chop and potato supper, the sun had disappeared over the mountain, but the sky still held leftover light, so we decided we'd take time to stretch our legs before setting up the tent.

"We'll see if we have any neighbors," I said, not quite liking the feeling we were all alone. The foray around the graveled road turned up no neighbors, nary a soul. City girl that I was, the lack of other humans gave me an eerie feeling, and either the quietness or the cool air set me shivering.

On our way back I noticed something odd about the dark green garbage cans and went over to one.

"What's the deal with the garbage can?" I asked as I thumped it with my knuckles and then lifted the top. "This thing is steel, and is square instead of round. Oof. I can barely lift this top. Why is the top slanted like that, I wonder?" I kicked the can with my foot and it didn't move a millimeter.

"Oh, they make them like that so the bears don't get in them."

"Bears?" I looked around anxiously, as though I might see one lurking behind a tree ready to pounce.

"Nothing to worry about," Fred assured me. "They're more afraid of you than you are of them."

I doubted that. We set up the tent, made sure our food was safely stashed (one of Fred's strict camping procedures) and turned in. No bear foraged around our campsite during the night, and the day dawned, with air so clean I felt that just standing there breathing would clean my entire body, inside and out. Squirrels chirruped, chasing each other up and down the tall Douglas-fir trees, trees in which the perching birds sang cheerfully.

Not in any particular hurry that morning, after breakfast I took a pad of paper and a pencil and walked to the edge of the creek. A tempting island stood in the middle of what I knew to be icy cold water. That's where I wanted to go, out in the middle of the creek, to sit down on that sun dappled, green island and write a letter home. Stones beckoned me to use them as a bridge of sorts, and I picked my route carefully, hopping from one to another. With one final jump I ended on the sandy beach successfully, my shoes dry.

This downed tree trunk will make a good backrest, I said to myself, and quickly sat on the soft ground, opened my notebook and started writing. Before I finished the first paragraph, which described the idyllic scene in which I sat, my subconscious kicked in. Did I hear something? Feel something? My scalp itched with anxiety. Did another camper move in during the night?

Someone was looking at me. I knew it. I jumped up and turned around. My heart and lungs started working overtime, big overtime. A huge, black bear stood on the other end of my little island. As I stared, horrified, he lifted his gigantic head and sniffed in my direction. Suddenly my fears about being eaten by a bear seemed close to reality.

I clutched the pad of paper in my hand and forgot about the convenient stepping stones. "BEAR!" I yelled as I sloshed across the icy water. "A bear!" I shouted at Fred, "There's a bear!"

Fred ran to see but only saw the bear's hind end retreating. I *had* frightened the critter just as much as he had frightened me. Every time Fred tells this story he says I sounded like a herd of horses galloping through that creek, and my eyes were round saucers. He also describes it as only a small, black bear. Ha. If it had been him face to face with that bear, *his* story would include a six foot grizzly.

Troy is about the farthest point west before Idaho. We'd covered what we wanted to see of Montana, other than to check out Hot Springs, a town a veterinarian in Kalispell had recommended as a possible place to set up a practice. Why not continue west and sightsee before we visited that small town and made up our minds? The Ford stayed on its western course.

Remembering my first sighting of Idaho's Coeur d'Alene Lake and its pristine beauty, still makes me smile. And when I see a picture of me sitting up in my sleeping bag on the banks of the Columbia River, I can feel the quiet, and see the majestic river flowing by.

We visited Coulee Dam, which interested me, but didn't make an indelible impression. Money running short and a decision to be made, we stopped our sightseeing and drove back to Montana.

***

Hot Springs is set in a valley between foothills. The valley is quite dry, sagebrush and greasewood the prevalent plants, the surrounding hills brown most of the year, with the green, forested Rocky Mountains in the distance. Hot Spring statistics informed us the valley was home to a vast number of cows, most of which the ranchers took to the surrounding mountains for summer pasture and back to the valley in the winter.

"They'd calve in the valley," said my new husband. "Most of the work done on the cattle would be in the spring, fall and winter."

We talked with the county commissioner, Mr. H.E. Smith.

"Yes," he said. "We have to go to Ronan to find a vet and that's a long way, so it'd be nice to have a local vet. But, I don't think a veterinarian could make a go of it here. Just not enough business."

Other people in the community agreed with his assessment.

Fred decided we had seen enough, and pointed the yellow and white Ford back to Minnesota. Had he made up his mind? I wondered, staring out the window.

"Well, what do you think?" he asked me.

"I don't know. The people in Fairview seemed to be the most enthusiastic about us coming," I hedged.

"I think we should try Hot Springs."

And he went into the discourse about the statistics. His decision stunned me. Why Hot Springs? No one we talked to thought a vet could make a living there. The town didn't appeal—it presented itself as a dumpy, "has-been" of a town. At one time people came, if not in droves, in respectable numbers, to take the hot, mineral baths and soak in the mud like a herd of sows. Now it sat, full of run-down cabins. Even the bathhouse looked shabby.

However, something about it obviously appealed to this man I married. Maybe it was the challenge. Maybe it was the cattle population numbers. Whatever it was, I didn't argue, and by the time we hit Polson, I relaxed and decided to forget it. My dad's philosophy was, if things don't work out in one place, try another. I decided to make that philosophy mine.

Back in Minnesota we fit everything we owned into the smallest U Haul trailer: a bed, mattress and dresser (cast offs from my folks), my sister Doris' old stereo, our meager wardrobes, and a few odds and ends, including Fred's diploma. It didn't take long to pack and load up.

Because I had made a big break from home immediately after graduating high school, the goodbyes were not as bad as they could have been. My older sister, Doris, was in the ministry and away from home, little Carelie had been born after I moved to Minneapolis and was now just a toddler, more like a niece to me than a sister, as I had not been with her much.

We made a last visit to Jennie, Fred's mom, and headed out the door, with her lamenting as we went, "Montana. You might as well move to the moon. I'll never see you again."

In Hot Springs, we looked at a grand total of two houses, the only two located out of town which had corrals and were available for rent. We settled in a small farmhouse belonging to N.G. LaRue. Mr. LaRue owned the local mercantile store and several properties, and, as no bank graced any of the town's streets, he served as banker for the area, loaning money to whomever he felt was a good risk. For thirty-five dollars a month, we rented the house and had the use of the corrals for any large animal veterinary work the ranchers brought to us.

A covered porch stretched across the front of the white, two-story house and added a certain pizzazz to the entrance, but, like many country houses, it had been sited so that getting from the driveway to the front door was awkward. The driveway ended at the back door, so everyone parked there, banged through the screen door of the side porch, and tromped across its creaky wood floor, all of which so effectively announced their arrival, I'd meet them at the kitchen door.

Fred liked the fact that, even though there was a long driveway into the yard, the house was visible from the highway, convenient for all our future clients. After we unloaded our few possessions, the veterinarian/carpenter immediately started the conversion of the downstairs bedroom into a clinic by building wooden shelves, sawing diligently with a hand saw.

Tilting my head, I smiled as I looked at those shelves. "Those corners are not exactly mitered," I commented.

"You want to try it?"

I backed away. "You're doing fine."

Two dog cages came next, the open door fronts which he stretched with wire and framed with boards. A couple coats of bright, white paint covered up most of the rough spots of his carpentry and it all looked pretty good.

He ordered a new surgery table and light, then called the salesmen of a few veterinary supply houses, who gladly came to fill the fridge with antibiotics and vaccines, shoving aside our milk and catsup. We were in business. Broke maybe, but in business.

Missoula, the telephone directory informed us, had an unfinished furniture store, and we squeezed out enough money to drive down and buy an unfinished desk, which I sanded and varnished and placed in our small living room. One rocker and one Swedish style chair joined the desk, so we did at least have a place to sit. People started stopping by to meet this new vet who thought he could make a living here.

After seeing our sparse household effects, many of the curious people who visited found things in their own households they didn't need any longer. Zella Smith, the county commissioner's wife, discovered an old kitchen table in their garage, so she invited me for coffee, after which we manhandled the table onto the top of our car, tied it down, and I drove nervously home, hoping our inexpert knots would hold. My next trip to Missoula I found and bought used kitchen chairs, and after a good sanding and a light green stain, table and chairs matched.

Our landlord saw me at the laundromat and brought out a washer. A young man wearing jeans and a baseball cap rather than the normal cowboy hat, stayed to visit a while after Fred vaccinated his dog. Maybe he noticed the hand-sewn patch on Fred's coveralls.

"Could you use a sewing machine?" he asked.

"I could make some curtains," I said with a smile. "I'd like a sewing machine."

That old Singer helped me make blue, checked kitchen curtains, and maternity clothes when I outgrew my skirts. After Jill's birth, Mr. LaRue saw me hanging out diapers and decided he could spare a used dryer for his rent house. The little white house filled with furniture and kids—three of the latter in three years.

The bridegroom and bride seeking their fortune turned into a man and wife seeking serenity amidst animals, diapers, phone calls, toys, and bills, and fighting a constant battle with dog hair, mud, blood, and manure.

PUZZLING PARALYSIS

Shortly after we started our practice, the kitchen door slammed against the wall, making my new blue checked curtains swing, and a young man carrying a black dog exploded into our house/clinic

"My dog. She can't move. She was fine yesterday. What's wrong with her?"

"Let's look her over." Calmly, Fred took the dog from the distraught man and led the way to the examination room, gently laying the animal down on the table.

To me the long tail and thick hair coat indicated some sort of small spaniel, but my knowledge of dog breeds was minimal. When a kid I owned a dog for a year, and had only slight acquaintance with a few others before marrying this tall, good-looking veterinarian who now examined the lifeless-appearing pet.

I watched as he lifted the dog's long tail and inserted a thermometer. One hand kept the thermometer in place while the other stroked and reassured the animal.

"Her temp is normal," he said after he cleaned and read the thermometer. He then palpated the abdomen, checked the ears, the eyes, and opened the mouth to peer inside. I smiled to myself when I realized I expected to hear, "Say ahh."

Something had completely paralyzed the dog. The only thing she moved was her eyes, which looked puzzled and apprehensive as they followed Fred's movements. Completing the examination, my husband also looked puzzled.

"I really can't say what's wrong," he told the owner. "Would you mind if we keep her until tomorrow and observe her?"

As he watched Fred examine the dog, the man had gradually quieted. "Please keep her and do whatever's necessary." He pumped my husband's hand firmly, his eyes as grave as his dog's. "My name is John Wright. The dog is named Blackie. She's a wonderful little pet, and we'd hate to lose her. Will you call me tomorrow and tell me how she is?" His forehead still creased with worry, he stopped at the desk and gave me his address and phone number.

Fred continued parting Blackie's hair, checking for who knows what, and muttering under his breath. "I can't think what could be the problem. She looks perfectly healthy, but can't move and I don't know why." Sighing, he laid the limp dog down in a newspaper-lined cage, and went to the living room.

With shelves for his textbooks and class notes still in the planning stages, he lifted each box of books from the stack in the corner and rummaged through, selecting several large volumes and many manila folders of notes. Soon notes and books were strewn around our brown rocker, Fred deep in his research.

"Nothing I find quite fits the picture," he said to me a couple of hours later. "We could send her to Dr. Brogger in Missoula for tests but she doesn't seem to be in distress. I'll think about it today and see what tomorrow brings."

The next morning Fred quickly checked the dog over, finding no change in her condition. Before leaving the house on his rounds, and still looking mystified, he told me, "Take her outside once in a while and set her down on the grass. She's housebroken and will be more likely to urinate when she's outside."

Several times that sunshiny morning I took Blackie outside, laid her on the grass, and patted her glossy coat as she looked up at me piteously.

"I'm sorry, girl. Fred doesn't know what's wrong yet, but he will soon." I continued to talk to the dog as I hung washing on the clothesline.

At noon Fred laid the dog on the examining table, determined to find a reason for the paralysis. His hands probed the spinal cord from neck to tail. I heard him talking to himself.

"Some dogs with long backs hurt their vertebrae, paralyzing them. But this is different. This is a total paralysis." Suddenly his hands stopped and he parted the hair, excitement lighting his eyes.

"Hey, Georgia. Look at this tick! This dog has tick paralysis!" I bent over and saw a huge, engorged tick.

"Ugh, look at the size of that thing. It's nearly the size of an acorn." I shuddered. "How are you going to get it out?"

"Usually you can just pull, if you're careful." Long fingers pinched hard around the partially embedded tick and he pulled slowly. Out came the monster.

"I wonder how I missed that before. I thought I'd checked every inch of her." His fingers continued searching the thick coat but found no additional ticks.

"Why would a dog get paralyzed by a tick? Don't lots of dogs get ticks?"

"Yes, but sometimes the toxin from the bite affects the dog. Blackie should get better soon, now that the tick is out." He put the dog back in her cage and left on the scheduled afternoon ranch calls.

An hour or so later I opened the cage, picked up the unresponsive animal and brought her outside, laying her gently on the grass. She was still, only her eyes blinking in the bright light.

"You'll get better soon, Blackie," I told her. "I'm going in to get another load of washing."

The phone rang as I walked into the house, so I answered it, then put another load of wet wash into the wicker basket.

"Hey, Blackie, how're you doing?" I asked, as I toted the basket to the clothesline. "Feeling better yet?"

Setting the basket down, I looked around, startled. There was no small, black dog anywhere near the clothesline.

"Blackie, where are you? Here Blackie."

What happened to her? Did she drag herself off? Was it possible she'd recovered that much so soon? I'd have to tell Fred I'd left her by herself. For such a short time, though, and she couldn't walk, she just stretched out on the grass, not moving. What would we tell the owner?

I forced myself to be calm. She hadn't been stolen, so she must be around somewhere. But where? My eyes searched the yard for possible hiding places. I walked around each of the two willow trees and found nothing except a few twigs, which every little breeze tugged from the tree and threw down for me to pick up.

"Blackie, here Blackie," I continued calling, and heard the nervous agitation in my voice.

Tall grass grew along the fence in the front yard. Maybe she hid in that grass. No. She couldn't go that far, I thought, as I hurried over to check. I crawled along the fence line, parting the grass beside and between each fence post. Stomach jumping with anxiety, I worked my way toward the corner. I'm getting too far from the house, I told myself, she couldn't possibly be here.

As I started to get to my feet, something bolted out of the grass. My head went up and I felt a sharp pain–one of the barbs from the fence scraped my scalp. I rubbed my head and talked to the offending rabbit who looked back at me from the shelter of a greasewood bush.

"I'm looking for a dog, bunny, who must not be around or it wouldn't be me who scared you."

Glancing around, I could see nothing moving other than a few grasshoppers who jumped and crawled up my leg. I brushed them off, then called again, "Blackie. Blackie. Here girl."

Rubbing my eyes like a baby just awakened from a nap, I trudged toward the house. Fred trusted me to take care of that pet and I failed miserably. He'd be disappointed in me. We needed to attract clients, but everyone in the community would soon learn I had lost Mr. Wright's dog. Fred's reputation would be ruined before he had a chance to prove himself.

Lost in my wretched thoughts and calling to the dog, desperation making my voice shrill, I put my foot on the first porch step. Something wet nudged my bare ankle. Startled, I jumped, turned and looked down.

"Blackie, it's you! Where were you?" The little dog pranced around my feet as I talked, giving absolutely no evidence of ever having been paralyzed. I scooped her up in my arms, burying my wet face in her abundant coat. The sun shone brighter, as I walked into the house and deposited Blackie safely in her cage.

The pleasure I received from calling the delighted owner helped me recover from the fright of nearly losing his pet.

THE COWBOY AND THE GOOSE

Cowboy boots beat a quick tattoo on the wooden porch floor. I opened the door and felt the expression on my face change from cheerful to apprehensive.

"I need a bottle of penicillin," was Paul Howser's greeting. "Think you can handle that?"

"Come in, Mr. Howser," I said. "I'll get you a bottle."

"Suppose you'll charge an arm and a leg," he grumbled.

Paul acts like he's in a hurry. Maybe he won't take time to interrogate me, I thought as I pushed the milk over and took penicillin from the refrigerator.

City-bred, I knew nothing about ranch life, cows or calves. Neither did I know anything about veterinary medicine. Even the names redwater, blackleg, brucellosis, and leptospirosis had just appeared in my vocabulary.

The entire ranching community knew Paul Howser. Like me, they were aware of his quick temper, his nosiness, and his know-it-all attitude. Paul, a trim man, and cocky, like so many short men, dressed in western shirt and jeans, boots and hat like the other ranchers. But, while most of our rancher clients respected the fact I had a lot to learn, and made allowances for my ignorance, Paul loved to intimidate me.

Well aware of my inadequacies, he especially liked to rave over the superior intellect of Angie, the wife of Dr. Ray Reed, a veterinarian who practiced in Lake County, just east of us. She knew everything and gave out advice freely, particularly if the advice included something she could sell. I didn't know Angie, but I hated her guts.

"What's the best treatment for scours?" Paul asked me now, and I noticed with dismay he leaned against the doorpost. It looked as though I was in for the usual grilling.

"I don't know for sure."

"Angie sold me some neomycin. That worked pretty good. You have neomycin?"

"Fred probably has it in his truck." I had no idea if Fred had it in his truck or not, having never heard of neomycin.

Paul had his "how dumb can you get?" look on his face, and I could feel my cheeks turning red. "Doc keeps tellin' everyone there's vibriosis in the herds around here. What makes him think that?"

"You'll have to ask him, Mr. Howser."

"Young whippersnapper. Coming in and telling us we have vibriosis. Angie and Doc Reed don't agree with that." Paul's voice and color rose. He pushed himself from the doorpost, pulled out a chair and proceeded to torment me for the next half hour. By the time he left, I was shaking and close to tears.

When Fred came home I complained again about Paul's relentless cross-examining. "You'll learn what's necessary, Georgia. Give yourself some time." He gave me a hug, then said, with emphasis, "Angie isn't a veterinarian and should not be giving veterinary advice."

***

My education about ranch life, veterinary medicine, and marriage continued through the next few years. My husband and I worked together well, and in spite of the tension involved in a busy veterinary practice, enjoyed one another. My confidence increased with my knowledge.

I was washing surgical instruments in the new clinic, which was adjacent to the house, when Fred banged in the door. Turning, I noticed he carried a large gunny sack.

"Open a cage door, will you?"

"Okay."

I ran into the next room and opened a cage, which he promptly filled with a huge gray goose. The goose made a few contented goose noises and surveyed its domain calmly.

"What's the deal?" I asked.

"It's a present from Orville Branson. Remember him? He's a polled Hereford breeder at Belknap. I'm in a rush. Have to go to Lonepine and will be home late. Maybe you'll kill and clean it. Just chop off his head. He'll make a wonderful Thanksgiving dinner." He saw the shocked, "I can't do *that*" expression on my face. "You'll do fine. He's a quiet goose."

Fred left, leaving a trail of goose feathers on his way out the door. I knew nothing about killing a goose. Chop his head off indeed! How could I hold that monstrous bird and simultaneously chop off his head? The nerve of that man. I'd cook Thanksgiving dinner, but I sure as shootin' wasn't going to kill and clean it too. In a fury, I turned back to the sink, washing, rinsing and throwing the instruments on the drainboard, saying angry, unkind words to my absent husband.

The door opened. It was Paul Howser.

What a day, I thought. A goose to murder and now Paul. I think I'll use the ax on Paul and save the goose.

Paul immediately saw something had made me lose my cool.

"What's wrong, Georgia?" He turned and listened. "What's that noise? What's in there?" His obnoxious nosiness getting the better of him, he opened the kennel room door and peered in.

"Doc starting in the poultry business?"

"No, Doc just flew in the door, dumped the goose, told me it

22

was Thanksgiving dinner and that I was to kill and clean the thing. I know nothing about killing and cleaning a goose and I don't intend to learn."

Paul looked at me, then glanced at his watch. "I have to run into town. I'll be back in a half-hour. Fill the largest kettle you have with water and have it boiling when I come back."

He was out the door. As I waited for the water to boil, I mulled over what I knew about Paul. People had told me he could change personality and be kind, but he never gave me any slack. Would he come back and take care of the goose? I doubted it. He *had* almost looked sympathetic, though.

In a half-hour, I heard a truck drive up. Paul strode into the clinic. "Where's your ax? Out in the shed? I'll get the goose. You bring the boiling water out, okay?"

Quickly I ran into the kitchen, grabbed the water and followed him.

"Here. You hold the goose like this." He stretched the neck of the mildly protesting goose, and made one quick chop. I shuddered but held tight to the goose until he took it from me.

"Now we just dip it in the water and strip the feathers off. See how easy it is?"

His hands quick and competent, he soon had the feathers picked and the entrails on the ground. He handed the plucked and cleaned goose to me. "You don't have to tell Doc I did it. Just pretend you did. He won't know the difference."

"It's not a patient, Dr. Bevins, it's a gift!"

Dr. Robert M. Miller cartoon

REMINISCING WITH BETTY CROCKER

When I won the 1958 Betty Crocker Future Homemaker of the Year award my senior year at Roseau High School, it flabbergasted Mom.

"However did you do that, Georgia?" she asked. She knew I refused to sew and only went into the kitchen when forced.

"Common sense. The test asked simple, practical things, just the opposite of what Miss Dahlquist teaches." I mimicked the home ec teacher's sweet voice, "'Okay girls, after you pour the liquid into the measuring cup, place it on a level countertop. Then stoop to eye level to see if the liquid is precisely to your measuring line.' Geez, you'd think it was a scientific experiment rather than a white sauce."

General Mills awarded me a pin and a cookbook. The chunky pin, a house engraved inside a heart, the heart dangling from a sheaf of wheat, was designed by some New York jewelry designer. I promptly stuck it in the miniature cedar chest the Lane company gave all the senior girls. It's still there.

The cookbook developed into a family treasure. Years of hard use tattered its red and white Scandinavian motif and disintegrated the spine cover. Many pages flap around loose, nearly illegible.

Betty Crocker did what Mother couldn't do, she enticed me into the kitchen. The food photographers at General Mills shot some fantastic photos of layer cakes. Even the names intrigued me: pink azalea, daffodil, old Kentucky nut, chocolate joy. My dad loved cake, and I loved the pictures.

I promptly walked to town, bought three layer cake pans, and baked my first layer cake. I piled rich filling between each layer, then smeared icing over the sides and top. Seven minute icing is supposed to be soft and lie in artistic whorls. My icing turned hard and shiny as sleet-covered snow with lopsided drifts. Dad didn't care. He ate my cakes until I left for the Twin Cities to seek my fortune.

Within two years I met and married Fred, and we moved to Montana. Betty Crocker rode in the U-Haul, along with our other meager possessions. As soon as I unpacked her, my husband picked her up, perused the table of contents, and slyly told me, "Most vet's wives I know make their own bread." Later I realized this remark was a ploy. He liked homemade bread.

Seven times I read the cookbook diligently; seven times I followed directions carefully, and seven times we could only eat the top half of the loaf. The bottom was heavy and yucky.

"I think you're kneading it too much," my husband said helpfully.

I ignored him but finally realized that Betty Crocker, like my old home ec teacher, was being too exact. I disregarded all Betty's instructions and pictures of how to mold a loaf of bread. Instead I rolled the warm, yeasty-smelling dough between my hands, slapped it a few times, like slapping a newborn baby, and popped the loaf into the pan. Common sense made for consistent success.

Cinnamon rolls and Swedish tea rings came next. Every baking day the ranchers and drug reps gathered in the kitchen of our rented farmhouse. They ate sweet breads and drank coffee as they waited for my husband to come cure their cows or buy their wares. The Pitman Moore rep remarked several times,

"Georgia, I can smell those cinnamon rolls the minute I hit the curve by the Niarada store. Makes me keep swallowing my saliva."

I basked in the small degree of fame my baking reputation brought me. Betty Crocker was my key to learning all the neighborhood scandals from the ranchers and all the gossip about other vets and their wives through the drug reps.

Though I continued to bake bread and rolls, when our children started arriving, Betty Crocker's cookie recipes got more and more popular. It's easy to tell our favorites. The snickerdoodle and molasses crinkle pages are not only taped, but are smudged with drops of an indeterminate liquid spilled in essential places. Perhaps it's drool from the kids, who were always at my elbow.

"Snickerdoodles, fun to say – to sniff – to eat," one of the kids would say, reading the heading. "Can I roll them in the sugar and cinnamon?" Together we'd take out the big yellow bowl, add the glossy white shortening, dump in the granulated sugar, and crack a couple eggs on top, a terrific color and texture combination: Yellow and white, glossy and rough.

Our family ate lots of stews, soups and pot roasts, simple foods that satisfied us and did not get completely ruined while we waited for Fred to come in from the clinic or home from a ranch call. By the looks of the cookbook, meat loaf was a standby in the old days also. The page with that recipe is half missing.

On the Thanksgiving day that Fred afflicted me with a goose, I arose early. I read and reread Betty Crocker's advice on cooking fowl. Instead of Biblical, "Thou shalt nots," she listed do nots. "Do not add any water! Do not season outside! Do not prick skin! Do not cover! Do not overcook! I wondered about the "Do not cover" part, but bravely set the goose in the roaster which I shoved, uncovered, into the oven.

That was a mistake. For three months afterward every time I turned the oven on, goose grease leaked out the door, and an oily, rancid butter smell filled the kitchen. I tried every cleaner I could find and spent hours scrubbing. Each time I got down on my knees in front of that oven, my respect for Betty Crocker's advice waned, and my anger at Fred surged. Nevertheless, in spite of some disappointment and some temper, we've enjoyed over fifty years together, Betty Crocker, Fred and I.

November 12, 1960

Dear Mom, Dad and Carelie:

   Fred's out tending to a sick cow this evening, and I'm sitting here on the little wood stool between the oil burner and the wall. Even though the stool is hard, it's part of my personal cozy nest, necessary as this old house lets in lots of cold, fresh air.

   There's a wind blowing tonight, but this morning it was calm and clear so I enjoyed my walk down the long driveway to the mailbox. The cold made my cheeks red and my fingers tingle, even though the sun shone so brightly the frost-laden trees dripped.

   About ten this morning, old John McCoy came over with another stack of books. Do you remember me telling you about him? He's a retired school teacher who lives, "down the road a piece." Ever since he found out I like to read, he comes every week or two with books. He sits and has a cup of coffee with me and we discuss the ones I've just read. Today we discussed "Not As a Stranger." It's a book about a young boy's quest to be a doctor. Without a library in town, having a friend like Mr. McCoy is a bonus.

   There's also a retired rancher, Mr. Ekblad, who must have every book Zane Grey wrote, and he brings some to me every once in a while. I'd never read Westerns, but I'll read most anything. I must admit I skip most of the descriptions about purple sagebrush and landscapes.

   The big news at this house is that I've finally learned how to bake bread! The first seven (yes, seven) times we only ate the top half of every loaf as the bottom was heavy and coarse. Fred kept encouraging me to continue. Today I baked two loaves of white bread and a pan of cinnamon rolls. The bread turned out light and delicious and the cinnamon rolls disappeared.

Dale Balison is the main reason for the disappearing rolls. He drives a fuel truck and keeps a schedule. When it's time for our oil tank to be filled, he comes without being called, usually timing his visit to coincide with afternoon coffee time. The oil tank is located right outside the kitchen window. With a fresh cinnamon roll aroma wafting from the kitchen, Dale made haste to join me for a cup of coffee and a roll. He didn't stop at one. The rest Fred and I ate at suppertime.

Fred always teases me about my male friends (all old, by the way) but a few women come and chat also. Anna Kemp comes often. This afternoon she stopped for a bottle of penicillin and we visited over a cup of tea. She likes to talk about the old days in Montana. Anna, a frail old lady whose husband died ten years ago, now runs the ranch herself. I said she is frail, but she really isn't frail at all, she only looks that way. Seven gates block the road between her ranch and the highway. That means seven times she stops, gets out, opens a gate, gets back in her pickup, drives through, stops, gets out, closes the gate, gets back in her pickup. Fred wishes she'd have cattle guards put in, not for her sake but for his!

A half hour or so after Anna left, Zella Smith called to talk but didn't come out. She's the one who gave us our kitchen table shortly after we moved here. She's a short little lady who always wears high heels, higher even than my highest heels.

"I had a stroke a couple years ago and Dr. Campbell told me I'd never wear high heels again," she told me. "I sure proved him wrong."

I've never seen her in flats.

Zella is going to sponsor me so I can join the woman's club in town. They call the club the ONO Club which means "Our Night Out." Zella says the club serves no good purpose, it's just a time when the women can visit. As you know, I'm not the most outgoing person on the block, and this will be a way to get acquainted with the women in town.

The dog we spayed after supper is stumbling around in his cage, recovering from the anesthesia. I'm learning how to help with surgery. I restrain the dog or cat while Fred gives it the anesthesia, tie the legs down so the animal is in the proper position, and hold instruments when he needs an extra hand. And, of course, I wash and sterilize instruments repeatedly.

Lights are coming up the driveway, and it's probably Fred coming home. You can see my day has been full. You might be bored reading all about it, but I am pleased with my friends and my accomplishments, and Fred is proud of me.

Tomorrow I know there will be a letter from you telling me about your day. I look forward to those letters as I feel a long way from home. Keep them coming please —

Your daughter, Georgia

DIVINE GUIDANCE

"This next case is a prolapsed uterus," Fred told me as we sped down the highway. We were barely more than newlyweds. I usually helped around our home/clinic, but that day my boss decided I should see the other side of his practice.

"One thing is critical in this business," he lectured as we drove. "You have to have the confidence of your clients. They have to believe you gave the right diagnosis and treatment regardless of the outcome."

Fred stopped talking when we turned off the highway onto a gravel road, and from there to a two-lane dirt track. I felt my eyes grow large as I saw old machinery, rusted barrels, heaps of tires, discarded refrigerators, and other junk lining the driveway. We pulled up to a rundown farmstead, with an older couple waiting beside the barn. Fred jumped out of the truck and started opening doors on the mobile unit, selecting the drugs and instruments he needed.

"We didn't think you was ever coming!" were the first words out of the woman's mouth. I studied her, marveling at her ragged pants, oversized blue plaid shirt and a denim jacket held together by large safety pins. Her husband looked similar, except he had a gray shirt and a brown, greasy cap perched on his head.

"Sorry, Agnes," my husband replied diplomatically. "Jim Andrews had a cow down, and . . ."

"Yeah, the cow's in here," Agnes interrupted, as she headed into the barn. There we found a Hereford cow with a prolapsed womb the size of a 50-pound feed sack hanging from her rear. I was flabbergasted. All I could think was, *How in the world is Fred going to get all that back inside her?*

"Get a bucket of warm water," Fred ordered. When I returned, he started to wash dirt and straw off the exposed womb. I jumped to hold the dirty tail out of the way.

At that point, the old woman bowed her head, raised her hands and reverently intoned, "Holy Father, this cow is in bad trouble and needs Thy help. Please guide Doc's hands so's he does right by her. Please, God Almighty, make it all go back in—and stay there. Thank you. Amen."

I stood and stared at Agnes. Her husband leaned against the shed wall, chewing on a straw, and my husband ignored everyone and worked on the cow. Finally I realized I stood with gaping jaw and closed my mouth.

It took time and consummate skill, but Fred worked the uterus to the point where the intestines inside it slid back into the cow's abdomen. The collapsed uterus was much smaller, but it still looked too large to go through the vulva. With Fred patiently pushing and prodding, little by little the womb disappeared into the cow. When he finished, we all let out a collective sigh of relief.

Agnes again took up her prayerful stance and said, "Our Heavenly Father, we thank Thee that Thou has seen fit to allow Doc to push all that back into that cow. Amen."

I handed Fred suture and needles and he sewed the vulva together so the cow wouldn't strain and eject the whole mess again. While I collected instruments and emptied the bucket, he injected the cow with antibiotics.

Agnes added, "Thank You again, Almighty Lord. As the Good Book says, Thy mercy is past finding out. Brood over this cow and make her well, so's we can breed her again."

As we rumbled away down the dirt road, I remarked, "Well, husband of mine, you've apparently failed with that client."

"What do you mean? That cow will be as good as new!"

"You told me it's important that your clients have complete confidence in you. But Agnes obviously has none at all, and believed that only divine intervention could save that cow." I couldn't help smiling, as I glanced over at him.

He laughed and said, "I guess you're right. When one of her critters dies, she blames me. When it lives, she gives credit to the Almighty."

"Does her husband ever talk?"

"He talks a mile a minute, when his wife's not around." Then, after a couple thoughtful seconds, "But I've never heard him pray."

"Did you pray like I asked you to?"

Dr. Robert M. Miller cartoon

HILLTOP RODEO

On a warm, spring day I stood looking out the window, wondering if the grass needed mowing again, and saw Fred's truck come up the driveway, followed by only a small puff of dust. Apparently he was not in his usual rush, as normally the dust billowed behind him, making my stomach knot up when clean, damp clothes hung on the clothesline. I knew he had been to Bob Craft's place to treat a "downer" cow. That's one term even I understood; any cow unable to get up was a "downer."

Fred slammed the truck door, collected a pail of dirty instruments, and meandered slowly to the house. An IV tube trailed from his back coverall pocket, and a smile flickered around his mouth. I wondered what happened at Craft's to amuse him.

When I answered the phone earlier that morning, I'd heard Bob's deep voice say, "I've a downer here, and it's my orneriest critter. That cow don't like nobody. When she's well, she'll take off after anyone within a mile. This morning she's layin' there, and when you come near, all she does is glare at you and swing her head. Won't get up."

He continued, "This cow is ornery, but she's my best cow, always high on the mountain eating the most lush grass. The other cows are too lazy to climb up there. Because of the good grazing, she always brings the biggest and fattest calf home in the fall. Can Doc come?"

I'd heard the best cow refrain often. Whenever a rancher called me with news of a sick cow, he always said it was his best. They all think the vet will drop everything and rush right over. Bob would have cause to worry, though. His was a shoestring operation, and a dead cow might make the shoestring snap.

"What are you smiling about?" I asked as I opened the door.

Fred handed me the pail and unzipped his coveralls, stepping out of them as they fell to the floor. Then he sat down on a kitchen chair and stretched out his long, blue jean clad legs, ready to tell me a story.

"As usual," he said, "the cow was not in a convenient location. I stopped at the house and Bob and his son, Jack, jumped in my truck. They directed me and I drove as close to the downer as I could, got out my stethoscope, thermometer, some calcium, and an IV tube, and we hiked up to the critter. Have you ever seen Jack?"

"No, just Bob."

"Jack doesn't really walk. He sorta lumbers along. He's an awkward teenager, six foot three or so, with long, skinny legs not completely under the control of his brain. Nice kid, like his father."

"Just a minute. Let me get rid of this bucket," I said, already in the pantry alcove where I set it down with a clang. Washing instruments could wait for a while. Back in the kitchen, I, too, took out a chair and settled down to listen.

"I examined the cow, told Bob it looked like milk fever, and if my diagnosis was correct, a bottle of calcium should do the trick. 'Milk fever?' Bob says. He takes his cap off and scratches his head. 'Thought only dairy cows got milk fever.' I explained to him that's not always the case, in nature and medicine nothing is ever 100%. Occasionally beef cows got milk fever. He was unconvinced, which surprised me. Usually he just takes my word."

Fred went on with his narrative. "Anyway, I told him if it was milk fever and we got some calcium into her, within a few minutes we'd know whether my diagnosis was right or wrong. If right, she'd be up and walking before we could get back to the truck.

He helped me tie up the cow–we put a halter on her, pulled her head to one side and looped the lead rope around her hind leg. Bob takes everything in, and I felt him studying this procedure. I put the needle into the jugular vein and held the bottle of calcium solution up in the air.

"While it dripped, Bob says, 'I've heard other ranchers talking about leptospirosis. Is that something I should be vaccinating for? When do you vaccinate, and what exactly is leptospirosis?' I explained the disease to him, what the symptoms were, and when to vaccinate. By this time the calcium bottle was empty, so I reached down and took the halter off.

"We stood around, talking about ranching, with Jack standing in front of the cow rocking back and forth on the heels of his new cowboy boots. Pretty soon I said, 'let's see if this cow's ready to get up.' I thumped her a good one on her ribs and she stood up, taking a few wobbly steps.

She then realized her strength had returned, and with this realization came rage and a desire for revenge."

"What did she do?"

"Like I said, Jack was standing in front of her. We were on the brow of a hill, with Jack between the cow and the steep side of the hill. She took off after Jack, who started to run, but too late. 'Eeeyii,' he cries. He continues screaming, the cow directing him down the slope with her head on his butt."

Fred stood up to demonstrate, spreading his legs apart and putting one hand on an imaginary cow's head behind him.

"Jack has one hand on the cow's head, his long legs pumping away a mile a minute. Hilarious. Bob doubled up, roaring with laughter. I joined Bob in laughing till my sides hurt. We had our private, wild cow rodeo event."

Fred stopped his story, laughing again at the memory.

"Did Jack get hurt?"

"No, there was a fence at the bottom, and he vaulted over that fence better'n any track star. The cow stopped at the fence and looked back at us. We skedaddled quick, I tell you. All Bob said was, 'Hey Doc. Looks like your diagnosis was right.'"

"Did you have to laugh at the poor kid? That cow could have done him in."

Fred smiled at me. "That's the culture of the Wild West, girl."

***

A couple of weeks later I sat at the desk, clacking away on the old Royal typewriter, as I worked my way through the monthly statements. Fred was out at the Craft ranch, taking a blood sample from a bull Bob had sold. We'd send the blood sample to the lab to check for brucellosis before the bull changed ownership.

A swirl of dust alerted me to the fact someone was arriving, and I caught a glimpse of Fred's red Ford truck with its new white, Bowie-Derr veterinary unit installed on the back. This unit had doors and drawers holding the necessary equipment for ranch calls, and a tank of all-important hot and cold water. Veterinary medicine could be a dirty business. The pickup's door slammed shut and soon the kitchen door opened. Fred stuck his head around the living room door where I sat at the desk. He was grinning.

"What's so funny?" I asked.

"Jack Craft."

"He get chased by the bull you were testing?"

"Nope. Jack had a bull riding adventure about as good as his cow riding one."

"Sit down and tell me about it."

Fred followed my suggestion and sat down on the brown, upholstered rocker, dusty coveralls and all. I hoped he didn't smell too bad.

"I stuck the blood tube and needle in my pocket and Bob, Jack and I walked over to the corral. The layout's about the same as most corrals—a long narrow alleyway leading from the corral to the squeeze chute. The chute has a head catch stanchion, and one side of the chute can be pulled in to squeeze the bull. Both of these are operated by pulling on ropes. Takes a little coordination."

I interrupted him. "And Jack, whose coordination is nearly non-existent, operated the ropes to both catch the bull's head and squeeze him, which have to be done quickly and pretty much at the same time. Right?"

"Right. It was a Black Angus bull, 700 pounds or so. He looked rather indifferent to me, not afraid. The not afraid part sometimes spells trouble. Bob and I hazed the bull down the alleyway, and he kept turning to look back, like he'd like to challenge our authority. But we got him into the chute and Jack pulled the rope that caught his head, and then pulled the rope so the chute squeezed and immobilized the bull, who didn't struggle as much as most do when they're caught in a chute.

"I put the halter on its head and pulled it to the side to expose the neck, collected the blood sample, noticing the bull had a belligerent look, but not thinking much about it. I stayed close to the corral fence."

"Then what happened?" I knew that wasn't the end of the tale.

"The critter waited quietly until Jack released the chute's side and opened the stanchion. Instead of running to the far side of the corral like most cattle do, he stood there for a second or two, then stepped out and quickly turned and charged Jack. Jack saw those 700 pounds coming and pulled frantically on the ropes to get up and out of the bull's way.

The kid didn't get up far enough, just far enough the bull could put his head under his rump. So there was Jack, sitting on that Angus, his long legs astraddle the bull's neck. The animal proceeded to toss his head up and down, which made Jack bounce like the ball of one of those paddle ball games kids used to play with. Jack was so busy hanging onto the ropes to keep from falling to the ground, he didn't let out a peep."

Dr. Robert M. Miller Cartoon

Smiling in spite of my concern for Jack, I asked, "How'd he get off?"

"The bull finally decided he'd gotten revenge and set the kid down, then trotted to the far side of the corral. Jack clambered out of there, uninjured, which is a marvel. Of course, his dad and I couldn't help but laugh at the whole fiasco. But we did wait until we were sure he was okay. I'm looking forward to my next call to Craft's."

March 13, 1961

Dear Dad, Mom and Carelie:

I have got to tell you what happened the other night. After supper Fred got a call. Martin Bjorge, one of the ranchers, had a cow calving. He'd been trying to pull the calf but couldn't get it out, so would Fred come? Fred donned his coveralls again, picked up the instruments I'd just cleaned from another calving, and left.

The rancher called from someplace other than home, as Fred told me they don't have a phone up in the foothills where Mr. Bjorge lives. I imagine it was about 7:30 or 8:00 when Fred left to go up there. At first I busied myself with a few jobs around here, then sat down to read while waiting. I read, and I read. And I waited, and I waited. I didn't know how far it was to the ranch, but I figured a half hour up there, an hour to pull the calf, a half hour back home. Ten o' clock came and went. No Fred. Finished with my book, I paced the floor, sat down in my corner by the stove, and continued waiting.

Eleven o'clock came and went. Twelve o'clock came and went. I'd get up and walk around to try distract myself with something, then sit back down. Surely it couldn't take this long to pull a calf! Maybe Fred ran off the road, killing himself. What would I do as a widow?

With no phone at the ranch, I couldn't call the Bjorges. We had talked about getting a two-way radio but didn't have the money. Who could I call? I needed to tell someone. Should I call the highway patrol? Or maybe Vic Holmberg or Dale Balison, who have been good friends, and whose gas station is where we get all our gas and our heating oil? My mind whirled around every which way, and I couldn't decide what to do.

Seeking for inspiration, I paged through the tiny telephone directory and read the entire thing in ten minutes. No bright idea came. If Fred had crashed down the mountain, they wouldn't be able to see that until morning. And what if I sent someone barreling to the ranch and he found Fred calmly helping with the second or third calving of the night? I'd feel foolish for calling and spreading an alarm. So I simply sat.

At 3:10 a.m. I saw lights coming up the driveway. Fred at last! I got up and met him at the door.

"Hey," he said, as he gave me a hug. "I thought you'd be in bed and fast asleep hours ago."

"I was worried about you," I said, near to tears. "What took so long?"

"Martin had tried to pull the calf, but when I put my arm in that heifer, I knew there was no way to get it out. So I had to do a c-section. I haven't done hundreds of c-sections yet so it went slow. While I stitched up the heifer, Martin took care of the calf, rubbing it down, and he saw the calf's tongue hanging out of its mouth.

"Finished with the suturing, I checked it out and found Martin had hooked the tongue with the calf puller and pulled– nearly slicing the tongue in two. The wound was so far back I spent hours stitching up that tongue. Talk about tedious! When I finished, Martin insisted I come in and have a snack."

We trudged up the stairs to bed, me vowing that never again was I going to wait up for my husband. I would go to bed.

Nothing else momentous has happened.

Love, Georgia

JILL

Parents expect great things from their first child. Perfection is not too high a goal. These misguided souls demand cheerfulness, politeness, eagerness to please and to top it off, insist on the first child being kind to any younger siblings who grab for their fair share of attention.

Jill reigned supreme for only fifteen months before being usurped from her only child, prettiest child, and smartest child queenship. But for those fifteen months she ruled with remarkable aplomb.

One of her subjects, Chuck Stipe, loved to engage Jill in

conversation, never mind the fact she only talked baby gibberish yet. He'd turn toward Jill, enthroned in her high chair, his black eyes narrating a conversation just as much as his voice. Jill, after listening intently, then took up her side of the conversation.

She leaned over her crumb-strewn tray, looked him in the eye, and jabbered. Finished, she threw her head back and laughed as though she'd told a big joke. Chuck then changed his tone and his facial expression to an argumentative one. Jill, meeting the challenge, changed hers also. No laughing now, this was a serious argument.

"Where's Jill?" we'd sing out as we tossed a blanket or clean diaper over our baby's face. By ten months she imitated both the words and our tone of voice. Because we made it so evident her first words delighted us, she continued to learn others.

The 50 mile trip to Stipe's house for Sunday morning meetings tested Jill's patience. To keep her in a good mood, I recited nursery rhymes. Sometimes I led. "One, two, buckle my shoe."

"Three, four shut the door," her little voice piped up from the back seat. Then we'd switch, and she would lead, and I'd reply.

In no rush to walk, our firstborn would sit on the floor and patiently drop pieces of wood into a plastic jar. "One," she'd sing out. "Two. Three. Four." On she'd go.

Jolene Jacobson, a friend and neighbor, came over early one afternoon. She lifted Jill up onto her soft lap, saying, as she usually did when half-lamenting her weight gain, "I'm in training to be a grandma, and grandmas should be cushiony."

With dark hair and eyes, Jolene had a smidgeon or two of Indian blood and the good looks that came with that bloodline. Jeans constituted the bulk, if not all, of her wardrobe, and, even though she was not a slim woman, she looked great in her preferred attire.

We visited over a cup of coffee, then she said, "Why don't I take Jill home for the afternoon? My Debbie and Jill are the same age and they may as well get acquainted."

Late that afternoon she toted Jill into the house, setting her down on the floor. Looking exasperated, she shook her head at me. "Did you know, Georgia, that Jill can count up to 15? You never told me that. She's barely 15 months old." She paused a second, then added, "At least Debbie can walk better."

In fact, Jill was barely walking at 15 months, just shortly before her little sister, Kay, was born. She had spent lots of time on the floor, mostly scooting around on her butt, as she never learned to crawl properly. Maybe she felt safer as low as she could get, what with the parade of people and animals through our kitchen.

The dogs were her particular delight. Whenever she'd see a dog being carried or led through our house to the back bedroom we'd converted to a clinic, she'd grin so hard her eyes nearly closed; her legs thumped the floor, and her arms waved enthusiastically in the air. All dogs not on a tight leash came over to inspect this whirling piece of humanity.

Counting and animals intrigued Jill. Camping did also. Even as an infant she loved to go camping. She would wake early and stare at the trees overhead, the dawning sun shining through and the breeze changing the patterns of the leaves. Fred would shed his sleeping bag, start a campfire and set a kettle of water on the flames in which to warm her bottle. On a later trip we took pictures of her after she crawled around in the soot and sand, engrossed in her exploration of this new environment so different from the clean and waxed linoleum of home.

***

Jill, sharing my lap with her unborn sister, laughed with me as I read her a book before bedtime. The book was titled, "Let Papa Sleep," and because of this book, Fred's name was changed from Daddy to Papa. As we enjoyed the book together, I worried, how am I going to love another child like I love this one? Young and inexperienced, I didn't realize a mother's love multiplies but does not divide.

When Kay entered our lives, Jill's status changed from only child to big sister. Even at the tender age of fifteen months, she understood you must handle babies of all descriptions carefully–a lesson learned from her proximity to multitudes of cats and dogs. As Jill sat by Kay's side, she'd uncurl her baby sister's fingers and gently touch her all over. As Kay grew and responded, Jill changed as well and gathered toys to share with the baby. Later, when Sue joined the crowd, both Jill and Kay did the same with her.

As time passed, Jill's inspection of her siblings and the animals which paraded through our kitchen expanded to include the scrutiny of any living thing she discovered. One day she found a large, fuzzy, yellow caterpillar in the backyard and wrapped it carefully in a piece of cloth. All day that caterpillar rode, wrapped up, on the back of her red tricycle, Jill getting down frequently to check on her prize.

"Time to come in, Jill."

"I have to get my caterpillar."

I watched as she picked up the snugly wrapped insect and walked with her pigeon-toed walk up the sidewalk, negotiating the two wooden steps with little difficulty, in spite of her eyes being focused on the small handful of cloth and fuzz. She walked across the creaky wooden porch floor and stood, waiting for me to let her into the house.

"Leave the caterpillar out here, Jill."

"It wants to come into the house."

I envisioned the caterpillar getting loose and hiding

somewhere I didn't want it to hide.

"It'll be fine out here on the porch, and it will be here tomorrow when you get up."

Reluctantly she laid her slight burden down in the corner by the woodbox and followed me into the house.

During the evening the caterpillar freed itself from bondage and crawled out into the middle of the porch, where Fred stepped on it as he came home from his last call of the day. Although I took away the cloth and her squished friend, hoping she wouldn't remember, my subterfuge didn't work. When morning came, she ran to the porch to check her caterpillar. So, at an early age Jill experienced death in the form of a squished fuzzy caterpillar and started her journey of enlightenment–Mom didn't always know what she was talking about.

***

All the dogs and cats in Jill's young life came and went with their owners, but it was a red letter day for her the day Fred came home with a golden retriever pup. When she realized this dog belonged to us, she'd grab that pup around the middle and haul it to the door every time someone came. "This is *our* dog," she'd announce. And so it was. "Our Dog" was the pup's name thereafter.

Jill did not just pat and rub Our Dog. She examined her. She'd lift her ears, open her eyes and mouth to check that all was well. I'm not sure how often she stuffed pebble pills down Our Dog's throat during treatment, but the dog never got sick, so the amateur ministrations did no harm.

Fred, of course, did not let his small, blonde assistant treat the client's animals, but whenever he put a dog or cat up on the exam table, here came Jill, pushing her wooden stool to the table. Up she'd climb, quiet and wide-eyed, as she watched him vaccinate, clean teeth, express anal glands–whatever was the show of the hour.

Her father put up with Jill "helping" and also managed to find time most evenings to play with her. However, during one period he simply could not; Western equine encephalitis was scourging the horse population, and he spent most of his days and evenings vaccinating or treating horses.

One evening after supper Jill saw him put on his coveralls, a sure sign of no playtime with Papa. She started to cry. I tried to explain. "Papa has to go and see some sick horses, Jill."

This did not console her. She flopped on the floor, shut her eyes and wailed. "Jill's sick. Jill wants Papa to look at *her*."

Her papa lifted her up and gave her a hug, then left. Knowing crying was no longer any use, our daughter wiped her eyes and sniffed her way to the toy box.

HEATED ARGUMENTS

After the Western equine encephalitis crisis passed, we took stock of our situation. We weren't only short of time, we were short of space. One refrigerator holding vaccines and antibiotics, plus our milk and eggs, had stretched to one fridge for clinic use, one for household use.

Even with those two old machines humming along, keeping their contents cool, gradually our milk and eggs were interspersed with Pitman Moore green vaccine boxes. And, though we kept kid's stuff to a minimum, we now were a family of five, another on the way. Fred started asking about land suitable for a clinic and a house.

We had lived in the little white house for five years, through good times and bad, warm times and cold.

Every winter, for the entire time we lived in Nobel LaRue's rental house, Dale Balison's red and white fuel truck made regular runs to fill the tank sitting outside our kitchen window. This precious oil flowed continuously into our brown, square, fuel oil burner, which crouched in our living room and drank copiously, giving us the dubious distinction of consuming the most fuel oil on Dale's route. And we didn't even try to heat the upstairs.

We'd bundle our two toddlers, Jill and Kay, and the baby, Sue, like Eskimos and tuck them into their beds at night. Some mornings I could take my fingernail and scrape off a quarter inch of cold frost pasted on the windows.

Sue, a chubby, healthy baby, possessed a robust cry. At naptime, if she woke before Jill and Kay, she destroyed the afternoon peace by waking them both. I learned to throw Sue's blankets over the oil burner to warm them, then wrap her up and tuck the bundle of baby and blankets out on the front porch in an old buggy we'd inherited from someone. It might sound inhumane, but the cold didn't seem to bother Sue, and she was seldom sick.

The hottest arguments in the house were over heat. If the oil in one tank got low, we had to go out and turn a faucet type valve to switch to the other tank. I've never been able to tell whether to go clockwise to turn a faucet off or counterclockwise.

One cold winter day I went out, checked, and knew I must turn the valve. Tentatively I turned it to the right a smidgeon. It turned. Then I turned it to the left a couple of smidgeons, and it also turned to the left. Whoever turned it last didn't turn it hard enough. Which way should I twist that valve? Was it counterclockwise? I mentally looked at a clock. Or clockwise? Why didn't it say "Off" or "On?"

After I turned it the way I thought appropriate, I shivered my way back into the house. My thought was not correct, I discovered later that night when the oil burner went out.

"Didn't you check the valve?" asked my husband, sounding slightly exasperated.

"Yes, I went and turned it."

However, I did not explain that it was only part way on or off or whatever and I didn't know which way to turn it. I should have confessed my dilemma, but Fred often gave me a hard time about being directionally challenged. Not only did I not know east, west, north and south, but even right and left gave me problems. He was older, way better educated and, to my mind at least, more intelligent. Why remind him of my disabilities?

Fred went out and came back, his face set. He jerked off his jacket. "You did *not* turn the valve," he said, too quietly, too calmly. Quiet reigned in the house. For two days I suffered through it, not understanding he wasn't mad about the oil burner going out, or at least not *that* mad, he simply thought I'd lied to him and it made him furious.

After I owned up to my shortcomings with the valve, things improved–until the boss of the household decided we needed some supplemental heat and brought a wood burning trash burner into the kitchen.

The trash burner itself didn't look too bad, just a white, enameled, rectangular box on legs, a black top with two stove lids, and one wire-handled gadget with a prong with which to lift the stove lids. The black, oily-looking stovepipe leading from the trash burner to the hole in the chimney, just under the ceiling, is what I absolutely hated. "Do we have to have that thing in here?" I protested.

"Absolutely. It's cold in this house."

I would rather have frozen than put up with that trash burner. The black stovepipe, the wood stacked behind the stove, the wood chips all around, the ashes, all irritated me beyond measure. The wood smoke smelled okay when fresh, but let it sit for a while and it gave off an odor that reminded me of the homeless bums' unwashed bodies in Minneapolis. Besides, in order to keep the thing burning, I had to stuff its gut every half hour. And heaven forbid if I should let the fire go out!

The plan for the new house John Williams contracted to build us showed a fireplace in the corner of the living room.

"No way," I told Fred. "No fireplace. Let's take that money and add a couple of feet to the two front bedrooms." We had fought so much about that trash burner he didn't even argue.

By the time John finished the new house, I was seven months

pregnant with our fourth baby, Joel. Fred hired Oliver Sederstrom, a rancher who did trucking on the side, to move us the five miles or less between the LaRue house to our new house.

Shortly after breakfast that Monday, pickups started coming up the driveway, the owners of ten-gallon hats jumped out, tromped up the wooden porch floor, and into the house. Instead of moving us with his truck, Oliver had put out the word to the neighboring ranchers, who responded en masse. They came with pickups, and each helped the other load.

Percy Cottet surveyed some of the boxes. "Didn't know you two were such heavy drinkers."

"No. Whoever would've thought," said John Welch.

"I'm just glad you men spend so much time in the bars. Makes more boxes for them to give away," I retorted, smiling at their teasing.

The girls and I left our good friend, Viv Coleman, at the house to catch any stray dust bunnies, and we went to the new house. One packed pickup after another came. I told the men where to put the boxes and unpacked as many as I could. It all went slick, even though emergency calls kept coming in and Fred missed out on the move, which turned out not only to be free, but a fun morning for all.

Jill, Kay and Sue loved the new place. Several times those first few weeks, I'd see them stretch their arms out and run down the hall. Freedom! This is when I realized how cramped things had become in the old farmhouse.

The girls loved the space; I loved the thermostat. It hung inconspicuously on the wall, but if I wanted the house warm, I pushed the little lever. If I wanted the house cool, I pushed the little lever. Magic. No valve, no wood, no stovepipe, and no ashes.

***

The normal nesting instincts of a pregnant woman kicked in after we moved into the new house, and I started gathering things for the expected baby. That consisted of going through stored baby clothes, throwing the ones too stained with milk and baby foods to put on a brand new infant, and filling in the gaps with unsullied things. A girl or a boy? That was the question. I limited the buying to clothes suitable for either.

It's special, having three little girls. Fred didn't seem to mind not having a son, but secretly I hoped this next baby would be a boy. I'd never had a brother, did not know what the, "Snakes and Snails and Puppy Dog Tails," part of the rhyme meant. It'd be fun to find out.

On June 10, 1966, a day after Jill's fourth birthday, Joel was born, an easy birth like his sister Kay's. The three little girls had a brother, Fred and I had a son. Instead of only lacy, girl socks to fold on laundry day, little boy socks joined the piles on the kitchen table.

To say that time flies fast or kids grow quickly, is a cliché but both are so true. Jill started first grade, a big step for any child, especially huge for the first in a family. A second child gleans school-savvy knowledge from the first. Kay had spent time as a "student" while Jill played "teacher," so knew all about school buses and teachers and fellow students and what to do if you have to go to the bathroom.

Jill enjoyed school so no, "I don't wanna go," problems surfaced. She started to read. All the kids loved to cluster around and listen to me read. Now Jill made a listener out of me, with both of us proud of her accomplishment. Through the years reading stayed Jill's passion, and every room in her house is crowded with well read books on dusty bookshelves.

February 21st, 1966

Dear Mom, Dad and Carelie:

I'm sitting here with thoughts of you, wondering how everyone is. How do you like school, Carelie? Have you been learning anything new and exciting? Do you have your tractor all primed and ready for spring, Dad? Mom, your letters are important. They keep homesickness at bay and shorten the thousand miles between us.

Spring is here, even though Mr. Winter is reluctant to leave. The reason I'm sure it's spring is that Fred converted our dog runs to temporary pens for scouring calves. Yesterday I went out to check on a sick calf, and in the process of leaning over the pen to hoist the critter up on its feet, I cracked a rib. At least it feels cracked. Laughing or sneezing is not to be laughed or sneezed at.

I poured Jill a bowlful of Rice Krispies this morning. When she heard the snap and crackle, she pushed it away with a look of disgust.

"I can't eat this. It isn't dead yet."

And our little Kay continues to be suspicious of the toilet. No matter how badly she needs to go, she stops and peers in. It's doubtful she's heard stories about crocodiles or rats coming up sewer pipes. She just checks for color; any hint of yellow in the bowl means she absolutely must flush the toilet before she can sit on it.

Oops. Someone's coming. More later.

It was a rancher and wife, Phil and Doris Pelley. Phil is so nosy. His eyes continually rove over the desk as he asks questions: Who has had trouble during the calving season? Is Doc busy? Are you selling much vaccine? He barely keeps his hands from riffling through the charge slips on the desk.

Both of the Pelleys smoke and they just flick the ashes on the floor. Phil goes as far as throwing his butts down and grinding them with his filthy boot. What class! Not my favorite clients. I suppose they wonder how we keep the practice open—goodness knows the business they give us doesn't help much. Oh well, most of our clients are great folks.

Time to get to work.

Love, Me

P.S. We haven't heard anything from Doris for a while, but I imagine she's busy being a dairyman's wife and a mother.

KAY

Parents expect a second child to be quiet, patient, uncomplaining, willing to accept second hand everything, and to top it off, resign herself to the fact the older sibling came first and is always going to be first. A second child, the parents feel, should be a follower of the older child, a leader of the younger. "Little Kay" or "Kay Kid," quiet, usually patient and uncomplaining, admirably filled her dual role as little sister and big sister.

The "Sugar and Spice and Everything Nice" part of the rhyme described her. Kay the feminine one, was sweet, quiet and shy, but also strong physically, and assertive when necessary.

Feminine though she was, she gave not a whit about her appearance. We took a great snapshot when Kay was six or so. She had pulled on an old tee shirt and shorts, yanked knee socks up primly past her knees, and stuffed her feet into her scuffed cowboy boots. A doll hung over her arm, a doll whose hair and clothes were strikingly similar to Kay's in style and class. I thought Kay destroyed the photo after she did get interested in looking her best, but she showed it to me a few years ago so it's still around.

One would think Kay would have been competitive—fighting for her place in the family—after Sue and Joel appeared on the scene. On the contrary, she seemed determined to just be herself and learn and do things in her own sweet time.

"Please pass the cherries," she declared plainly while we sat around the dinner table. There were no cherries on the menu and we passed the peaches to her.

"These are peaches, Kay, not cherries," we informed her. Her pigtails bobbed in assent, and she smiled her luminous smile.

The next day, same table, same time; "Please pass the cherries," Kay's voice piped up.

"These are pears, Kay, not cherries."

"Yep," she agreed. It didn't matter to her. As long as we set a bowl of fruit before her she didn't care what we called it. Was she telling us, "Don't make life so complicated?"

Complications came in earnest after Jill started school. Kay anxiously awaited the day she could get on that yellow bus and be a big girl also. But, whenever I suggested she learn her alphabet or how to write her name, she'd shrug her shoulders, look placidly at me and explain, "I'm only four years old."

Finally I'd had enough of the, "I'm only four years old" routine.

"Kay," I told her one day, "if you don't learn your alphabet and your numbers, you can't go to school. You'll have to stay home when Jill goes again." She hardly took time to think about that before running to fetch the Dr. Seuss alphabet book.

"Big A, Little A, What begins with A?" Our little daughter intoned with me, "Aunt Annie's Alligator . . ."or some such nonsense. We wrote big letters and small letters on notepaper and posted them all over the house. "What's this one, Kay?" we'd ask. Our second born found it wasn't hard after all. In fact I have a sneaking suspicion she knew most of them already.

Kay might not have cared about her appearance, or about being first in the learning department, but she knew how to manipulate the opposite sex even when a kindergartener. Every morning, when a neighbor stopped to pick her up, Kay deliberated at the house door until a curly haired boy jumped out and opened the back car door. Then, sweeping out of the house, she entered the car and settled majestically in the back seat. The boy shut the door and away they went.

It wasn't just kindergarten boys. Ready to leave the drug store, my arms full of packages, I instructed Kay, "Run ahead and open the door, Kay." Obediently she ran ahead, but stopped short of the door. A tall man stood nearby. Looking up at him, the small girl smiled sweetly. Immediately he opened the door. "She learned young," he said and winked at me as we exited the drug store.

***

Being the second child, Kay grew acquainted with hand-me-downs, both toys and clothes. With only fifteen months

59

difference in age, the same toys served both girls appropriately. That's not saying they didn't fuss over the favored toy of the day, but the little spats happened infrequently and passed quickly.

"That trike's too small for Jill," Fred told me as he came into the house. "I've been watching her ride, and her legs hardly fit under the handlebars. I'll get her a new one."

So Jill happily mounted a new tricycle and Kay inherited her old one, which didn't seem to bother her. They played together, riding up and down the driveway between the house, large animal clinic, and shed.

"Remember to put your tricycles away," we'd yell out the door when dinnertime or bedtime came. "Someone might drive over them if you leave them in the driveway."

Jill and Kay liked to drive their trikes down to watch Lewis Mountjoy weld the large animal clinic's railing along the loading dock. One evening he backed out of his parking place, heard a crunch and leaped out of his truck. Kay's tricycle lay there–all twisted out of shape. Lewis brought the mangled trike back to the house.

"I'm sorry. I saw the girls by the house, but should've looked more carefully for their trikes."

Profoundly thankful it was only the trike which he destroyed, I said, "Well, Kay shouldn't have left it behind your truck."

Kay did not cry but came close. The next morning, Lewis came to continue work on the railings. Instead of going directly to work, he lifted something from his truck and came to the house.

"Here's a new tricycle for Kay," he said, setting it down by the door.

A delighted grin from the pony-tailed blonde thanked him. Now she had a bright red trike, and it was newer than Jill's.

A problem did pop up with the not-so-new clothes situation. Every spring and fall I'd open closet doors and bureau drawers and drag out clothes. "This is too small for Jill. Does it fit you Kay?" Usually it would. So, instead of new clothes, Kay wore Jill's good, but second hand clothes. I'd worn hand-me-downs when a child and didn't think much about it. Until one day Kay came home from school, not crying but obviously upset.

"What's wrong, Kay?" I asked.

"A boy in school asked me if I ever had any dresses that weren't Jill's dresses," she replied, sniffing just a little.

"Oh. I see."

A small town, an observant child; things I hadn't considered. So the next time we shopped, Kay came home with some new dresses to add to her wardrobe.

A VARIETY OF GRANDMOTHERS

With grandparents, aunts, uncles and cousins all living far away in Minnesota, Grandma Jennie Alderink's visits constituted the bulk of our kid's involvement with relatives. Most people would describe her appearance as "old fashioned." It was obvious she made her dresses, you'd wonder wherever she found such practical, laced up shoes, and she slicked her salt and pepper hair back into a severe bun.

Jennie came once a year and stayed a month. I kept busy in the clinic and she helped with the baking, cooking and mending. Her accusation that I saved up a year's worth of mending for her was nearly correct. During one of Grandma Jennie's visits, Jill came into the room where she sat sewing.

"If you give me some suture, I'll help you grandma," she volunteered, a statement which told she seldom saw her mother using sewing thread.

Jennie's help freed me enough I could spend time drinking coffee and visiting with her about relatives and friends, a relaxing break, different from the normal coffee breaks with ranchers and drug reps. Whenever she ventured out to the clinic, she was pleasant and outgoing. People liked her. My relationship with my mother-in-law soured, however, when she started playing favorites with her grandkids, first preferring Sue over Jill and Kay, then transferring her affections to Joel.

One particular day I escaped for a quick trip to the store, leaving the kids in the care of their grandmother. Before I even opened the car door, I remembered the forgotten grocery list on the table, so I ran back to pick it up. In the minute or two I'd been out of sight, Jennie had turned on Jill and started bawling her out. It's possible Jill said something to her grandmother that teed her off, but she certainly didn't deserve the tongue lashing she was getting. I bundled up all the kids, except baby Joel, and took them with me.

One year, expecting Jennie's visit, Sue kept saying, "When Grandma Jennie comes I want to sleep in her room."

"Okay, Sue," we told her. "You can sleep with Grandma."

The anticipated visit came and the first night a pleased Sue pulled back the blankets and settled herself in Jennie's room. She surprised all of us the next night by jumping into bed with her sisters.

"Aren't you going to sleep with Grandma Jennie tonight, Sue?" her father asked.

"No."

Our three-year-old shook her head as she answered, setting her blonde hair in motion. "Grandma Jennie sleeps too noisy."

My folks visited occasionally, usually just Mom and Carelie. My mother was several years younger than Jennie, a little more modern in appearance, and with a lighter personality. Mom delighted in all our kids when they were small.

She sent large packages for each birthday; one year she even experimented with sending a cake. I don't remember how she packed it but I know it wasn't frosted and she tucked the candles in the side of the box. She wrote many letters and enclosed sticks of gum for the kids in every letter. But, by the time Jill and Kay were pre-teens, Mom changed her attitude. The reason? She thought the girls were not treating their little brother right.

Neither grandmother understood the sisters' excellent relationship with Joel. They would hear the arguments and assume the girls were ornery to him, when most likely Joel would have started the ruckus just to have a little fun with his sisters. Both Jill and Kay gave Joel lots of attention and included him in their lives.

It's a wonder Jill and Kay didn't retaliate on Joel for the favoritism the grandmothers showed toward him, but they didn't. Sadly, they never experienced the joy of having a grandmother who loved them without reservation.

Wes and Viv Coleman helped fill the grandparent role. When our girls were small they often invited all three over for a few days. As the Coleman's ran a pig raising operation, the sharp, nasal-clearing stench of the pigs, and the flies the smell attracted, made the farmyard an undesirable place. Neither the foul odor or the buzzing, clinging flies bothered the youngsters when Wes let them hold the enchanting, curly-tailed pink piglets.

Larry, Harley and Ruth, the Coleman teenagers, all liked little kids, but Harley was our girls' hero. When they came home and tipped their cereal bowls up to get the last of the milk, and I protested, they'd state firmly, "Harley does it." Or when they decided to put ketchup on everything they ate, "Harley does it." The days with Wes and Viv were special days. My little girls cried, not when I left them, but when I came to fetch them home–a fact which bothered me more than I wanted to admit.

None of them jumped up and down with glee when I'd pick them up from Bill and June Mercer's house either. Neither the million dollar view of the green Clarkfork River running below the property or the little more than a shack clinging to the mountainside in which Bill and June lived, interested the girls. What mattered to them was that Bill and June gave of themselves and their time to make their visit delightful. Again, as with the Coleman visits, I don't know all their activities, but I believe they spent most of the time outside digging in the garden with June and helping her do goat and chicken chores.

Our family never got away from animals. Besides the clinic animals and the menagerie at home, the Colemans introduced them to pigs and the Mercers to goats. The pigs wore a certain charm, but in my opinion the little goats had them beat in the cuteness department. Why is it we like things in miniature? A hog or an adult goat is anything but intriguing.

Trains excite nearly everyone. To the girls' delight the railroad tracks followed along the bend of the river down below Bill and June's barnyard.

"When that train whistle blows," June told me once, "whatever those girls of yours are doing, they yell at one another and race to watch the train. No matter how many cars that engine pulls, until they wave at the caboose they are transfixed." She chuckled and shook her head. "They'll even leave the dinner table."

And, all too soon for my beloved children, I'd arrive at the door to take them home, away from the train, the goats, and Bill and June. Home, where their loved but familiar menagerie waited. Home, where busy parents did not take time to answer every question, cook whatever young despots wanted, or tell stories about growing up with twelve active siblings whose mother cared not a whit about mud tracked into the house.

DRAINHOLE GOSSIP CENTER AND TONGUE DEPRESSOR SPLINTS

Until we could save more money to build a clinic, we decided to use the basement in the new house for that purpose.

"We need a concrete stairway from the garage to the basement," Fred told John Williams, the contractor. "It should be double the width of a normal stairway with low steps and good railings."

John look puzzled. "Why so wide?"

"So any client can safely carry their pet, or a calf, down the steps."

John also built a room downstairs to house the dog and cat cages, and put in a new sink and cabinet. The shelves Fred had laboriously built five years earlier, we set up on one end of the room, plugged in one of the refrigerators we'd also had in the rental house, and moved the desk and chair opposite the sink area.

Also, as instructed, John installed a drain between the desk area and the sink area. If he'd known what all would go on around that particular drain, he'd have had a chuckle or two, but at the time he had no idea that hole in the concrete floor was destined to be a community gossip center. And all because of sick calves.

Scours, a virulent form of diarrhea, hit newborn calves every spring, some springs worse than others. It was the bane of the ranchers. Not that it couldn't be treated, it could, and usually the treatment was successful. But, even if they injected the calves with antibiotics or pushed boluses down their throat at home, treating them consumed considerable valuable time.

They had to keep going out and checking the animals, catch the sick calves, either treating them out in the pasture or throwing them into the bed of their pickups and taking them in closer to the farmyards to be cared for. If they brought one in, the mother simply followed the pickup home. Sometimes the antibiotics weren't successful, and dehydration was the next problem.

That's when they decided it was time to see the vet. I'd hear them coming down the wide stairway sputtering and cussing because the calves in their arms would, likely as not, let loose with a load of diarrhea as they came. They'd push through the double swinging doors, stride to the drain hole, dump the sick calves on the floor and survey their dirty, stinky jeans with disgust.

"That crap has simply the most foul smell possible," Percy Cottet told me more than once, which was something I certainly agreed with.

Fred's first job was to tie the calves' legs together and lay them with their butts toward the drain, making their jugular veins available for IVs. He'd then get the IV apparatus out and start fluids dripping into the bloodstream. The ranchers' job was to hold the bottles of fluid up in the air and gossip with one another. It wasn't unusual to have three or more ranchers at a time sitting there. Nearly always Fred would leave on calls and I'd listen to the gossip and help switch bottles when needed.

Normal excrement from a bovine is malodorous, but calves' scours, yellow in color and thin as water, has its own, rotten, indescribable stench. The drain and a hose helped with clean-up, but the whole messy situation made jeans my uniform of choice.

My mom never believed women should wear jeans, and when she visited, I normally put on a dress to keep the peace. She ventured downstairs to the "Drainhole Gossip Center" once, and saw me in a dress among those ranchers. When I knelt to help with the IV bottles, my skirt decided the ranchers needed something to look at besides their sick calves, and pulled up indecently. I pulled it down. It pulled up. Waves of disapproval crashed against me from where my mother stood by the desk. Finally, giving a loud, "tsk, tsk," she disappeared up the stairs.

"You should wear jeans, Georgia, doing what you do," she told me later, voicing my exact sentiments.

Today's vet techs wear scrubs with monograms on the jackets or pictures of cute kittens and puppies. In rural Montana we all considered scrubs for medical doctors and nurses. Everyone else wore jeans.

**

Even Sylvia, the local beautician, wore jeans. Sylvia also wore a brightly colored smock, usually covered with either human or canine hair, and preferred pink, fuzzy slippers for footwear. Her hair was gray at the roots, an orange/red on the ends and frizzed all over. How any woman dared to have Sylvia color or perm her hair I found hard to comprehend. Yet many women did, and they looked quite presentable.

Hairdressing brought in the necessary money for Sylvia's living, her love belonged to her Pomeranians. Once she came in carrying a tiny Pom in her arms. It, like all of Sylvia's dogs, was meticulously groomed.

"Hi, Sylvia, what's up?" Fred asked.

"Miss Susie jumped from the sofa and yelped. She's carrying her front leg and it has a bend where there is no joint. It must be broke."

"Set Susie on the exam table and we'll take a look at her."

I held the delicate dog as Fred ran his fingers up and down the leg. "It's broken all right, but it's a simple fracture. We can fix it up. Hand me the clipper, Georgia."

Carefully and gently his large hands clipped the hair on the petite leg. "All there is between my fingers and the bone is thin skin," he remarked. "I can easily feel the break." He tore off a piece of adhesive tape from a roll and laid the tape lengthwise under and over the leg, pressing the two layers of tape together that extended beyond the paw.

With his bandage scissors, he cut a notch in the end of a tongue depressor, and put the tape into the notch. Next came cotton padding to wrap around the leg. He pulled slightly on the tongue depressor to put tension on the leg, reducing the fracture.

Nodding, he said, half-way to himself. "Yes, I felt the bone slip into place. Now I'll turn the tongue depressor and tape under the leg."

He straightened up for a moment, then wrapped tape around the tongue depressor splint and leg.

"All done. Let her go back to Sylvia."

During the procedure Sylvia had stood at the head of the table and talked quietly to Susie. The dog kept her eyes on her owner, but except for an occasional slight whimper, stayed quiet and still. When I released the Pom, she got to her feet and cautiously put her leg down. Finding it didn't hurt, she walked stiff-legged across the table. Sylvia picked her up and petted the small face.

"There now, Susie," she crooned to her pet. "All fixed up. Doesn't hurt much now, does it?"

In a normal voice she asked, "When do you want to see her again, Doc?"

"Three weeks, Sylvia. Make sure the splint stays dry."

The door closed behind her. "I could have sent her to Missoula," Fred told me. "They would have anesthetized her, x-rayed the leg and put on a patented aluminum splint. But an xray would not show any more than my fingers could feel, and a tongue depressor fits the front leg of a Pomeranian as good or better than a fancy splint. With a little care, the pain I caused Susie was minimal."

A Drainhole Gossip Center, jeans and tongue depressor splints. Not exactly high class medical standards, but it all worked. In a few years we had a new small animal clinic with a surgery, a pharmacy which we inelegantly called a drug room, a kennel room with stainless steel cages, enclosed dog runs, and an efficient large animal clinic. Nothing glamorous, just practical. About like us.

June 20th, 1966

Good morning to my Big Sister, Doris:

We received the fudge yesterday. Thanks for the excellent proof that you can finally make a good batch of fudge. All those Sunday afternoons spent wasting Mom's sugar finally paid off. Feel free to send any additional confirmation of your ability so we can make sure this wasn't just a fluke.

Fred and I had an interesting Sunday night a couple weeks ago. A rancher on the other side of Plains called, oh, about eight at night. He had a cow with a prolapsed uterus and asked Fred to come and put her back together. Jennie was here, (I wrote you that Fred's mom was coming to visit, didn't I?) and the kids were in bed, so Fred asked me to come along and help keep him awake.

Going out to the truck, Fred checked his supplies, and checked the gas gauge.

"Should be enough gas," he commented. "I could call Vic and he'd open the station for me, but I don't think that's necessary."

We tootled up the road, past Rainbow Lake and all those vacant miles between there and Plains, then traversed the gravel road to our destination. Fred stopped the truck at the house. The rancher came out saying, "I couldn't get her in, but she's quiet. Shouldn't be a problem."

Those words are ones Fred shudders over often. Why, if the critter is so quiet, couldn't it be brought into the corral? Our client climbed into the truck beside me and Fred drove through the gate and into the pasture. As feared, the cow was not where she'd last been seen.

The steering wheel kept the driver grounded, and the client clung to the door, but I, stuck in the middle, bounced up and down and sideways as the truck hit every high and low spot on the rough ground. Fred turned this way and that, trying to find his patient. No full moon lit the night, and the headlights only made a dent in the darkness right ahead of us. Fifteen or twenty long minutes passed.

"It's amazing how far she traveled. That prolapse should have slowed her down," Fred commented, a tinge of impatience in his voice.

Beside me, the rancher leaned forward and squinted through the windshield, "Hey, that looks like her, right there," he said, with relief. He pointed ahead and to the right of us. Finally.The men jumped out of the truck and approached the cow quickly but quietly. She didn't move, probably exhausted from her wanderings around the pasture.

Of course, there were no lights to conveniently switch on, so Fred left the truck running and the lights shining on the site. Putting a prolapsed uterus in takes a while in the best of circumstances, and these were not the best of circumstances. It seemed to take forever, and I thought longingly of home and bed way before the last suture was in. We cleaned up, put the instruments away, and went wearily out of the pasture and on our way home.

Yes, the inevitable happened. Too much wandering around in the pasture, too much running the motor to give light, so half way between Plains and home we ran out of gas, on that section by Rainbow Lake which sees no traffic after sunset, as no one lives there. No one.

"Now what?" I asked as the truck hiccupped a few times and rolled to a halt.

"I should have called Vic and had him open the station."

Fred stopped and thought, then continued, "I hate to do it, but guess I can call Mom on the two-way and have her call Vic."

So, in a half hour or so, here comes Vic, swinging cheerfully out of his truck, gas can in hand, and puts in enough to get us home. He then waves, says, "See you." and, "It's nothing. Glad to do it" to Fred's apology, and is on his way.

When the end of the month statement came from Vic, I perused it carefully but it had no charge listed for his midnight rescue with the gas can. Fred asked about it.

"No charge," Vic told him. "Those things happen."

Hot Springs is not the ideal place to live in some ways, but you couldn't find better people to work with.

I was going to ask a few questions about what you're up to now, but this has gotten too long. I'll write again.

Love, your sis, Georgia
Thanks for the fudge….

CAMPING VACATIONS

Everyone in the family liked the outdoors, so camping vacations were a natural. On some of our camping trips everything went as planned, and we all went home satisfied we'd had a good time. However, sometimes camping seemed only a matter of survival, and the most fun we had were the stories we told after we arrived safely back home.

The stories were better than the reality on one of our trips to Yellowstone National Park when our girls were small. Maybe Joel was a baby, or maybe I was pregnant with him. At any rate, it was in the 1960's.

When we entered the park, the weather was reasonably nice, and the only problem we had was our girls' obsession with bears. At that time, park personnel let the restaurant managers throw their leftover food in dumps, a bear magnet, and did not penalize tourists who fed the bears. As a result the park abounded with the animals, which excited our girls.

It made naptime for little Sue impossible. Bears kept jaywalking over the roads, waddling slowly from one side to the other. Jill and Kay could not be persuaded to silently watch them. Instead, every time Sue settled down and started to nod off, either Kay or Jill, or both, would shout from the back seat, "There's a bear!" And, immediately wide-awake, all Sue's muscles tensed as she jumped to see.

Then the temperature dropped and the rain started. Looking back I wonder why we didn't have the good sense to pack up and go home. It wasn't as though we had traveled across the United States of America to get there. Cold, rainy weather and camping do not go together.

Plus, on this trip we camped in tandem with our friends, Chuck and Doris Stipe, who owned a pickup camper. They wanted to move around from one campground to another, which forced us to put up and take down our tent in the rain. With experience came proficiency. Before the end of the trip we'd slam down the trunk lid, ready to move in the same time it took the Stipes to get their camper packed. This gave us a certain evil satisfaction, a "We'll show 'em," feeling.

After the Stipes left for home, we lingered to visit a small museum. The museum interested none of the girls, who were too young to appreciate history, but when Fred and I said it was time to leave, they all started crying. To go outside and start shivering again did not appeal to them. They wanted to stay where a furnace put out some heat.

Fred can remember one good thing about that trip; he caught fish, which is unusual for him. We hired a fishing guide and spent hours in the drizzling, cold rain while Fred fished, until finally even the guide decided enough was enough, and moved the boat to where he felt sure no fish would bite. Then, and only then, would Fred agree to quit fishing. The girls huddled under the prow of the boat and whimpered themselves to sleep. I felt like joining them.

***

We camped at Glacier Park, where we didn't get mauled by grizzlies, at Lewis and Clark Caverns, where we didn't crash down the mountainside on that makeshift, rickety contraption bringing us to the mouth of the cavern, and on the top of a mountain between Idaho and Montana, where we did get rained out in the middle of the night.

The moon and stars lit up the night sky, and we laid our sleeping bags on the ground, trusting the heavens' assurance it wouldn't rain. About midnight thunder and wind woke us, telling us we had misplaced our trust, and warning of a storm.

"Get up and run to the car, kids," Fred ordered, and they obeyed with alacrity, as we adults scrambled to get everything stuffed in the car—a Corvair, which, amazingly, held all the camping equipment, including the tent. That was one time I appreciated Fred's fussiness in keeping a neat camp, as in jig time we were down that mountain and into Wallace, Idaho.

Corporate CEO's who run establishments such as Holiday Inn and Super 8 turn up their noses when it comes to building motels in small, mining towns like Wallace, but downtown we found an old hotel.

Disheveled and sleepy, we barely noticed the hotel clerk escorting us to an open cage elevator and up to a suite of large rooms consisting of a parlor, two bedrooms, and a bathroom—a bathroom outfitted with the deepest claw-footed tub ever made. In the morning we put all three girls into the tub to wash and play. They could not see over the top of the tub, and we couldn't see the tops of their heads when we looked in from the bedroom.

In the light of morning, we explored the old hotel and took rides on the elevator, feeling like caged animals as we rode up and down. The next time we traveled through Wallace, we checked and found they had torn the hotel down in the name of progress. I always felt glad for the night that rain gave us a taste of antiquated hotel life.

***

Butterscotch, our golden retriever, accompanied us on nearly all of our camping trips, or on any hikes, such as the time we decided to find Banana Lake; a body of water Fred had heard about and never seen. He parked the car on the side of the road where he thought we should start hiking, and the kids and Butterscotch scrambled out of the car and into the woods. The dog, every part of her showing her delight at being let loose in the forest with her people tagging along, smelled water and headed straight toward it.

At the edge of the small lake, she stopped long enough for the girls to catch up, then plunged into the water. As she plunged, ninety-nine turtles woke from their sun-induced snooze and hurriedly slipped off their respective logs.

"You should have seen all the turtles. Millions of them," the girls yelled to us laggards, clapping their hands with excitement.

Butterscotch, paddling around in the water, turned and looked at the girls, as though wondering why they didn't come in and join her fun. Kay and Jill were not interested in getting into that uninviting lake filled with turtles, mud and green gunk. They hankered to fish. Between the disturbed turtles and the dog exercising her innate love of water, fishing did not go well. Only a few little fish lost their lives that day. But Butterscotch kept us laughing with her antics both in and out of the water; the sandwiches tasted delicious, and we were together, sitting in the warm sun.

***

The sun's heat didn't warm the air another time when Butterscotch exhibited her love of water. It was a crisp, fall day and the Martin Dykstras joined us in setting up camp on Thompson River, which was covered with a thin layer of ice. A bit of ice didn't deter the water loving dog, and soon she happily broke through and waded around, splashing like a barefooted kid in a mud puddle. Her fur-flinging showers, funny on a warm, sunny day, irritated all of us in the cold weather. Now the draw was a large campfire–not her joyous splashing.

Dykstras, who lived in Thompson Falls, had pulled Martin's small camping trailer, which he used when logging, into the makeshift campground, and our trusty tent waited in the trunk of our car. Fred checked the clear sky and left the tent in the trunk. He spread tarps and blankets on the ground, unzipped our sleeping bags and laid the bags and more blankets for a covering. Ten-year-old Wayne Dykstra wistfully watched from the sidelines. Finally Fred asked him, "Do you want to sleep with us, Wayne?"

"Mom, Dad," begged Wayne. "Can I sleep with them?"

After some cajoling, his parents agreed, and soon we all snuggled down under warm sleeping bags and blankets. The night turned colder and colder. Our family pet inched as close to us and our body heat as she could. When day broke, Wayne pushed his head out and saw frost on his sleeping bag. "How cold do you think it got last night?" he asked Fred.

"Oh, I'd say around zero."

"Hey Mom, Dad," Wayne yelled, bursting into their warm trailer. "I slept outside in zero degrees and there was frost on my sleeping bag!"

Butterscotch opened one eye and raised one eyebrow, Butterscotch style. She'd been wading in icy water and slept under the stars when wet. Zero degree weather? Piece of cake!

***

I often wondered about the work involved in camping. If we worked as hard at home as we did when we camped, wouldn't we feel ill-used?

The man of the house would clear the area where he intended to set up the tent, throwing any rocks, acorns or pine cones out of the way. With a grunt and a groan he'd lift the tent out of the one-wheeled Sears trailer where we kept all the camping equipment (after we outgrew the Corvair) and lay it out on the ground. After digging around in the trailer for the stakes and the hatchet, we'd all help set the stakes, giving them a good whack with the dull side of the hatchet.

As our tent was the old fashioned cabin type tent, putting the poles in was the hardest part. I rejoiced when Jill and Kay got old enough to take my place. Jill usually volunteered her services.

First, all the poles were laid out to see what went where. Thankfully we had color coded them to make that job easier. She'd crawl into the door of the tent, the weight of the canvas on her back, dragging the ridge pole and the end vertical pole with her, lift the tent up with her head, stick the end pole in place, raise the ridge pole, and put the end pole in the hole of the ridge pole. Holding the whole tent up, she'd work herself over to the door and set the second vertical pole in place and the other end of the ridge pole in that opening.

At that point Kay and Fred would maneuver their way in with the side poles and install them. If the temperature outside was hot, it was stifling inside the tent. It's no wonder we so often simply ignored the tent and slept under the stars.

Air mattress preparation came after the tent. At first we used my good set of lungs to blow up air mattresses, but it wasn't long and we purchased a simple pump which only made my arms ache instead of my mouth sore. After opening the sleeping bags and fluffing up the pillows, the inside of the tent looked cozy, all ready for a good night.

By this time everyone's appetite was whetted and our attention turned to scrounging for firewood and hauling water from the closest spigot, jobs all knew were necessary before the cooking started. Kay and Jill managed those, with help from their father. I'd take out the groceries and cookware while Fred built up a campfire spot with rocks.

Cooking was an adventure itself, as we crouched over an open fire, smoke in our eyes. It was no big deal if something was a little too brown or a little greasy, the aroma and open air made anything into a gourmet meal. As the girls grew, they cooked and Fred helped. I'd clean up. Anytime I can get out of cooking I exult. After the meal, I'd fill a pail with water, find the pink plastic dish pans, soap and dish towels, and wash the dirty dishes.

After the requisite marshmallow roast, we set the trusty water pail on the rocks to warm up for the cleansing of our dirty bodies. We seldom camped at a campground with showers. The more warming of water, the more scrounging for firewood.

In spite of the work involved, the change from the duties of home and clinic made the time out in the woods enjoyable, even for me.

SUE

The baby in my belly kicked and squirmed. Rubbing tired eyes, I sat quietly, the small room enfolding me in its darkness. No streets lights shone through the un-curtained window, only the moon's weak light. Familiarity told me I faced the square, blond-finished stereo that sat in front of the window. To my right stood the new, brown sofa and to my left the wood desk we bought unfinished, and which had been my first attempt at sanding and varnishing raw wood. On each side of the window the outlines of two horse prints were visible, painter's tape doing double duty to both frame them and adhere them to the wall. Under my slippered feet I felt smooth, well-waxed linoleum. Everything was in perfect order awaiting the birth.

Susie Kammerer would need all her energy to keep the household running during my hospital stay. She would be responsible for our two small girls, the cooking and dishwashing, plus the telephone duties for the veterinary business. Our dear friend Susie knew what to expect, as she came weekly to answer the phone and do necessary chores, while I did the grocery shopping and ran errands in town.

In her 70's, Susie freely admitted to being no spring chicken, so keeping things shipshape for her felt important to me. Perhaps hard work caused my sleeplessness, or maybe the reason was an unusually active baby.

"If you're trying to get out, little one, kicking isn't going to help." I lifted myself out of the chair and waddled off to bed. Again.

This time I slept, but about an hour later awakened. Something was wrong. I turned in bed and felt wetness. "Fred," I whispered, "Either my water broke or I'm bleeding." Fred jumped out of his side of the bed and I rolled out of mine. When he turned the light on, we saw blood flowing down my legs and pooling on the floor. Too much blood. As I clumsily put on Kotex pads and clothes, Fred called the doctor and scooped up the sleeping girls. We headed for the hospital.

Dr. Campbell calmly examined me and reassured us. "You're not quite ready to give birth," he said. "We'll just put you in bed and elevate your feet." I lay there and worried about Susie and Fred's coping skills. Oddly, I felt no apprehension about the baby.

Two or three days later, Dr. Campbell discharged me and Fred came, took me home and left me with Susie while he drove his truck to Ted Mefford's to treat one of his Tennessee walker horses. It was noon, so I sat down with Susie and the girls to eat our lunch: tomato soup, cheese and crackers. Before I finished the meal, I felt the bleeding start again, and apprehensively packed myself with pads, muttering under my breath, "What in the world is happening? I didn't have any problems with my other two."

No one answered the phone at the Mefford's.

"Everyone's out in the corral, I suppose," I told Susie. "It's on the way to the hospital, so I'll stop by and tell Fred. He has a call to Thompson Falls, but if he knows I'm bleeding again, he'll come and find out what's up before he leaves."

"Why don't you call someone to come and pick you up?" Susie asked. "Maybe my Fred could come out." Susie had never learned how to drive.

"I'll be okay. It's not far."

Fred's truck sat in front of Ted Mefford's corrals, and I saw activity by the chute. Not daring to get out of the car, I honked the horn. As soon as Fred saw the car, he came over. "I'm bleeding again and on my way to the hospital."

"I'll be there in a few minutes."

The nurse put me to bed, elevating my feet. When Fred came and saw me, not in the delivery room but in the exact position as before, he decided he may as well leave for his next appointment in Thompson Falls, 50 miles away. Later Dr. Campbell came in to examine me. "The placenta is coming before the baby. We need to do a c-section. I'll have to talk to Fred." He called and received permission to operate.

Sue was truly a beautiful baby, chubby, pink cheeks and blue eyes. No birth canal trauma marred her in any way. The date: February 16, 1965.

But things were not so beautiful for me. Every time I moved I hurt. Tentatively I touched my skin and heard it crackle under the surface.

"It's gas that's collected during surgery. Move!" the nurses instructed. "The more you move the faster it will disappear."

My husband agreed with them. "You have to get rid of that gas and the only way is to keep shifting positions." If I stayed immobile, I felt okay, when I stirred the least bit, I felt pricked by hundreds of sharp nails. When the gas finally dissipated, I started throwing up.

A c-section on a cow is no big deal. She'd be up chewing her cud before the calf dried off. Fred didn't compare me unfavorably with any of his patients, but yet I felt humbled. Jill and Kay popped out with no problems. This ordeal taught me to sympathize with other women who experienced difficult births.

As I couldn't nurse Sue while sick and she refused a bottle, the nurses fed her with a dropper. When they started bringing the baby to me to breast feed, Sue was not used to working for a living. She wanted sustenance poured down her throat. She screamed. I cried. Finally we reached a truce, and she reluctantly accepted a bottle.

It was an uneasy truce. When Sue was old enough to smile and laugh, she responded well to Jill and Kay but not to either Fred or me. Neither of us could coax a smile out of her easily, though she'd cuddle and be content when we held her.

If she felt like crying, she let loose with her whole being–long and hard with a low-pitched voice. The little girl looked like a Gerber baby, a picture of health. Colic is normally the culprit, but it didn't look as though her tummy hurt. We almost came to the conclusion she liked to hear herself whoop it up, as she continued to be cranky much past the normal colicky age.

***

Our fourth baby, Joel, was born 16 months after Sue. Our busy lives got even busier. Maybe the answer to Sue's war against the world was simply not enough attention. Ruth Coleman came and stayed with baby Joel, and we took the three girls to Portland, Oregon, which was a vacation for the family females and a working vacation for the family male, as Fred attended the American Veterinary Medical Association convention there. I spent all day every day with the three girls, and our unhappy third child completely changed her personality. From a fussy baby and sober toddler she turned into a sweet, loving little girl.

Expensive, downtown hotels were not the normal for us, but this time we lived it up. Maybe the girls weren't as impressed as I was with the brass luggage carts shining in front of the hotel's glass doors, the doorman with the equally shiny buttons on his uniform, the lobby carpeted in deep pile, the elevator which hummed us up to a large room with two huge beds, but I was awed. My background did not even include a motel of any kind until after I graduated high school.

In all this luxuriousness, knowing my only responsibility consisted of taking care of our three little blondies, I felt almost dizzy. Absolutely nothing else distracted me; no phones, no ranchers with muddy boots, no dogs and cats to treat, no bookkeeping staring at me from the desk, no meals to cook.

After Fred left the next morning, I led an exploration of the hotel, feeling like a mother duck with three ducklings trailing me. On the top floor a swimming pool invited us to get wet, but it disappointed all of us when I realized even the shallow end was too deep for the ducklings.

"We want to go in, Mommy," Jill begged, her voice echoing in the cavernous, chlorine-smelling room.

"You'll have to take turns."

"Okay."

So I set two kids on the side of the pool, where they competed in a game called, "Who Can Kick the Most Water?" while I swam and played around with the third.

The days passed quickly, and it wasn't hard to entertain the trio. Even walking down the sidewalk in Portland was an adventure for them. When Fred finished his day he'd come back to the hotel and take us out to restaurants; dining establishments we ordinarily didn't even look at, much less eat in. Maybe the hostesses and waiters cringed when we walked in, but many times we heard compliments such as, "Your children are so quiet and respectful," or "You have such a nice family." I loved it, and realized we took our kids' good behavior as a given.

Portland's Chamber of Commerce booklet informed us about their zoo, so we either stayed an extra day or Fred took a day off and went with us. A miniature train clicked clacked its way around the zoo, discharging passengers here and there. Between the train, the exotic animals, and chasing the chickens around in the petting zoo, which was Sue's favorite part, the girls had a great day and so did their parents.

It doesn't take long to get used to the good life. On the way back to Montana we stopped in Idaho for a meal. The three girls ran to the café door, opened it, and piled in–they were familiar with the routine. Except this was a small hole-in-the-wall diner in a rural Idaho town, not a big city restaurant. They all climbed up onto the wooden benches in the booth and one of them remarked loudly, "This chair is hard." The waitress came with water glasses and another child looked incredulously into her glass.

"There's no ice in my water," she complained.

"These are paper napkins," said a third little girl.

Ah yes, girls. Back to the realities of small town life.

***

Perhaps it was all the crying Sue had done when an infant and toddler that helped make her strong. She walked at a younger age than her sisters, rode the plastic horse on wheels quicker than they did, and mastered the art of trike riding sooner than either of the other girls. Not only did she spend her days in constant physical activity, she was sturdily built like her mother. When I'd lift the kids from their bath, Jill and Kay felt insubstantial in my hands while Sue was solid and muscular.

As every family member and most acquaintances know, Fred is obsessed about obesity. He called Sue his "little fullback," but she was not obese, she simply had more body mass than either Jill or Kay. When her papa saw her eating more than he thought she needed, he'd ask her to sit next to him at the table. If she wanted seconds he'd give her green beans instead of potatoes, salad instead of casserole. She thrived—she must have gotten ill occasionally, but I don't remember it.

Sturdy described Sue's doll also. Our girls did not lack in either toys or pets, but Fred didn't believe dolls were necessary. One Christmas I put my foot down, and we got both Kay and Sue dolls. I believe Jill wanted an erector set that year. Sue's tow-headed, pink-cheeked doll with a chubby tummy did not get cuddled like a baby. She'd grab a hank of its hair and drag the doll along after her. I hope that doesn't reflect on my parenting skills.

Tow-headed, pink-cheeked Sue may not have had an affinity for her doll, but one day she felt a kinship with a chimpanzee. Even in Hot Springs, Montana, posters proclaimed in large red letters, "The Circus Is Coming to Town!" Town meant Missoula, not Hot Springs. Hot Springs had a grand total of 631 people while Missoula was a small city. I took the three girls to Missoula, all of us excited. I'd never been to a circus either.

We sat on a bench directly in front of the middle ring. The action in three different places proved impossible to take in: bareback riders, a lion tamer insisting his lion sit on a stool while the lion growled and showed his teeth, jugglers doing fantastic feats, elephants, and clowns. And over all the action we could hear the tinny music. Even the smells overwhelmed us: the warm urine from the animals, the sawdust, the popcorn and hot dogs.

Years later when we took our grandchildren to the rodeo in Springdale, Arkansas, Austin, around four years old at the time, watched the cowboys play Cowboy Poker. After the cowboys put their hands on a table set up in the middle of the arena, the rodeo clowns let a bull loose. The cowboy who kept his hands on the table the longest would win the game and the purse. Austin watched intently, but the action was too fast. When the bull sent the table flying through the air and the cowboys beat a retreat to the fence, the little boy yelled, "Do it again. I didn't see it all."

That's exactly what I felt like at the circus. Sitting in front of the middle ring I could keep track of that, but missed the action in the two side rings. "Do it again," I wanted to shout, "I didn't see it all." My little charges must have felt the same way, as their heads swiveled frantically left to right. Finally we all gave up trying, relaxed and just watched what was in front of us.

Then the young chimp came in. His antics are what Sue remembered and chattered about for a long time. The pajama-clad animal turned off a lamp, jumped into his tiny bed, pulled up the blankets and settled in, apparently for a long sleep. Then, all of a sudden he threw off the blankets, jumped out of bed, pulled a pot from under the bed and sat on it.

"That monkey's going potty!" Sue cried. Instant empathy. She knew all about that routine, having been potty trained herself in the not too distant past.

***

One of our youngest daughter's little quirks involved the regular bathroom and the half-bath by the kitchen. She always washed her hands in the half-bath but went to the full bath to go potty. One particular day, during dinner she excused herself, ran back to the bathroom to go potty, then skipped merrily past the table to the half-bath to wash her hands.

"Hey, Sue. Why didn't you wash your hands in the other bathroom?" I asked. "There's a sink in there too."

My voice wasn't accusing, but maybe the fact we all smiled made her think we laughed at her. At any rate, her blue eyes welled up with tears, and I realized how easily her feelings could be hurt.

Looking back, I know I wasn't as sensitive to what any of the kids felt as I should have been. Patience has never been one of my virtues. It is true that with four children in the house and a business adjoining, obedience was important, but it probably wasn't as essential as I thought. Occasionally I spanked my kids, and then often regretted it afterward, although my rationale was that a swat on the bottom cleared the air quicker than did a "time out."

I remember giving Sue two spankings. Before we sowed lawn seed at the new house, Fred ordered several loads of sandy soil to put on top of the hard clay. All of this sand had to be raked level. Fred worked on it every chance he had, and I also spent some time raking sand whenever I could find a few minutes.

The girls played quietly in the living room one afternoon and Joel slept in his crib, so I ran out to rake, leaving the door ajar so I could hear the phone. Sun beating down on my head, I raked diligently until some sound or movement made me look up. There was a lineup at the living room window—three little girls watching their mother work in the heat. I waved and smiled at them, until I noticed Sue chewing on the window sill. It was just the right height for her to clamp her sharp little teeth into. I threw down my rake and stormed into the house.

"Sue," I yelled, "You're ruining the wood." I grabbed her and delivered two swats to her backside. One reprimanding word would have sufficed.

Another time the towel rack over the tub was her undoing. Because this was the main bathroom in the house, and the only bathtub, we needed several towel bars instead of the measly single one in most baths at the time. On a shopping trip to Missoula I found the perfect towel rack, one with room for several towels. It looked similar to a ladder and attached to the wall. I blanched at the price tag, but bought it anyway.

One evening I put the girls in the tub where they played and soaked for a while. When I came in to scrub them up, I found Sue had climbed onto the edge of the tub and was hanging on to the new towel bar with her hands, her feet dangling. The bar sagged in the middle and we never managed to get it straightened. What I considered permanent disfigurement of objects was not nearly as enduring as the marks on my heart later.

Athletic little Sue gave us a scare one morning. This was before we remodeled the garage into an office, and the three girls and I gathered on the little porch between the garage and the kitchen. We waved goodbye to Fred as he backed his truck out. When we turned to go back into the house, Sue, perched on the top porch rail, lost her balance and fell solidly on the garage floor, which was about a five foot fall. She landed flat on her stomach.

I bounded down the porch steps, adrenaline surging, and knelt by her side. Just as I felt to see if her heart was beating, she gasped for air. The breath had been knocked out of her. But was she injured? Internally, maybe? I radioed Fred, and he turned around and came back. He examined his little daughter and declared her fit, then left. She soon played as though nothing had happened.

Sue loved old people, and that included an old, arthritic minister, Charlie Krub, who often stayed in Hot Springs to enjoy the hot mineral baths for which the town was named. He rented one of the numerous small cabins in town. Charlie believed the hot mud and water relieved his arthritis, and he tried to stay the 21 days the bathhouse advertised as the best bet to cure you of everything from arthritis to warts.

My private opinion was that 21 days sitting in a moth-eaten cabin in the dull town of Hot Springs might make you physically better but would do a number on your mentality, so I often invited Charlie over for meals. He never refused an invitation, and usually stayed throughout the evening, eating popcorn with all of us.

Often Marlene Sederstrom joined us. Marlene was a high school student, a favorite of the family. She often babysat our kids, or worked around the house, and she loved Charlie just like our kids loved Charlie. All of the ministers who stayed with us while having gospel meetings in the area had been women, Charlie was the only male minister with whom our kids grew well acquainted.

Every year we attended our four day church convention at Ronan, which was only over the hill as the crow flies but took us about an hour to drive. At the 1968 convention the congregation gathered for the services each day, but, instead of sitting quietly, whispered together until the service started. When the usual three ministers (all men) rose, walked up on the speaker's platform and took their seats, the audience quieted down.

Before one meeting a minister chastised us for not coming into the meeting at least 10 or 15 minutes before the service and sitting reverently until the service started. The next meeting Sue sat on the end of our bench, right on the aisle. The newly chastised congregation sat still and quiet, the chairs on the speaker's platform still empty. Puzzled, Sue looked down the aisle at the platform, and in a loud, clear voice said, "Where are all the Charlies?" That sent a titter through the congregation.

She made people smile another time. Like Jill, Sue was pigeon-toed and wore white, high topped shoes on which we put braces at naptime and bedtime. Finally the orthopedist gave us the go ahead to buy them dress up shoes. To Missoula I went, three little girls in tow, and we bought black patent leather shoes with straps for Jill, Kay and Sue. All of them were pleased, but I will never forget Sue running ahead of us down the sidewalk, tossing her head and delighting in her new footwear.

Years later, at a writer's meeting, the lecturer asked us to write a poem, something I had never done. The following is my first poetry writing effort.

FOR SUE

I have a picture in my mind
a small girl
running, shaking her head
feeling the wind through her blonde hair,
feeling the sidewalk under new, shiny patent
leather shoes.

Passersby look, then glance at me,
her pleasure mirrored in their eyes.

I have a picture in my mind
a small mound
decorated with flowers already wilting
in the warm summer wind
and surrounded by pretend grass hiding the
disturbed earth.

Passersby look, then glance at me, with my
grief echoed in their eyes.

When writing this memoir, I asked Fred to write about his last vivid memory of Sue. This is what he wrote:

A week before Sue's death we went to Charlo to watch the Fourth of July fireworks with Chuck and Doris Stipe and family. We made sure we got to the park early to let the kids play, and I pushed Sue high in the swing. At three-and-a-half the little girl was fearless. I would get in front of the swing as she came down, then leap out of the way just before she slammed into me. She squealed so loud with delight that people watching thought she was screaming with fear.

This family picture was taken shortly after the Fourth of July.

Fred, Sue, Joel, Jill, Kay, Georgia

***

On the day of Sue's death the yellow climbing rose by the front porch opened its first bloom, which we all went out to admire. The morning sky was blue and cloudless. I felt quietly happy that morning, the house looked neat and clean, and the kids were playing contentedly while I did bookwork downstairs.

Jill appeared in the doorway. "May I go get the mail, Mommy?"

Hesitating, I considered her question. Our children had always obeyed our instructions to stay in the yard, not to go down the driveway toward the highway. Because Jill would be catching the school bus soon, I had been taking her with me to the highway to get the mail, teaching her to look carefully both ways before crossing the road to the mailbox. Traffic was normally light on that stretch of road going to town, but not everyone obeyed the speed limit.

"Yes," I told her. "You may go." And I went back to my task. What I didn't realize was the two younger girls followed Jill. There was a package jammed into the mailbox, and Jill couldn't dislodge it. She called Kay to come and help, and together they pulled the package out. About that time Sue decided to join her sisters.

Downstairs, I had hardly picked up my pencil when a terrible premonition hit me. I couldn't even feel my feet as they hit the stairs. Just as I passed the kitchen window, I saw a small body fly through the air and knew one of our girls had been hit by a car.

Running out the door, I screamed, "Don't move her, don't move her. I'll call the ambulance," to two men who were running toward the ditch. In my frenzied state, I still could remember first aid instructions about not moving the victim. Inside, with my hand on the phone, I realized the community had no ambulance. I called the hospital anyway. Did I hope someone would come?

The men didn't listen to me, of course. One of them picked her up and a car roared up the driveway. He clambered awkwardly but quickly out of the car and put Sue in my arms, then opened the back door and gestured to me, "Get in, we'll go to the hospital."

I felt Sue's unresponsive weight momentarily and handed her back. "I have three little ones here. You'll have to take her. Go. Hurry."

While I held her body in my arms I did not notice any injuries, but after my two girls and I entered the house and I had called Doris Stipe, I noticed the red blood on my green dress. Doris ran out and told Fred, who was at their place pregnancy testing cattle. He must have found the 50 miles between the Stipe ranch and home a long drive that day.

Pat Managhan, our nearest neighbor, came over immediately when I called, and she stayed with Jill, Kay and Joel, while I drove the short distance to the hospital. Maybe my frenzied phone call did help, or maybe it was coincidence, but Dr. Campbell met me in the hospital hall. He told me Sue had been killed instantly. My brain knew this, but my heart wasn't ready for the knowledge yet. A person hopes for a miracle. This was not the time for a miracle. I drove home and radioed Fred, afraid he'd speed and have an accident. There was nothing he could do anyway.

Like most accidents, this one could easily have been avoided. The road was straight, the visibility excellent. Most people, seeing two children on one side of the road and one on the other would have hit the low, gentle ditch. Dr. Campbell had told me the driver of the car was Alex Morrison, the Sanders County attorney. Later I learned the man I thought a passenger was the driver of another car who had seen Alex hit Sue and stopped.

Some things are foggy about that terrible time, but I clearly remember Jolene Jacobson. Jolene was in town when she heard what happened, and came right away, even before Fred made it home. I had flung myself on the girls' bed and heard her ask Pat, "Where is she?"

I sobbed out to Jolene, "He hit her. Just like a dog. She flew through the air just like a dog." Jolene had seen Alex and tried to tell me he was distraught over the accident, but that did not mean anything to me.

When we were arranging for the funeral, Pat Managhan called. She did not say, "What can I do?" She simply stated they were bringing chairs over. "You'll need them." She had gone through it. Everett and Pat had lost a college-aged girl in a car accident a few years earlier.

A simple-minded character in one of, was it a Toni Morrison book? greeted any new acquaintance with the words, "What is *your* tragedy?" Not many people get through life without at least one tragedy. Our family is not unique.

Fred arranged for the funeral to be held in the school multi-purpose room, which filled quickly. We brought all three of the kids with us. Because of the unsightliness of Sue's head injuries, the undertaker suggested a closed casket. Apparently when I saw her right after the accident, the trauma to her head did not yet show.

There were many flower arrangements and wreaths, but the only ones I remember are the casket cover the local florist made, a blanket of tiny pink roses which draped softly over the casket, and a small white basket of pink roses sent by the Diehl family in Plains.

Our minister, Everett Wilcox, spoke at the funeral. Carol Erickson of Missoula sang Hymn 34 in the hymn sheet and sang every word distinctly and beautifully. As we don't have the hymn in our book today, I'll type it in here.

> One day He took a little child,
> And set it in the midst of them,
> To show the perfect citizen
> Of Holy New Jerusalem.
>
> So beautiful that little child,
> Obedient to its Lord's request,

So unaware of pride of place,
So sure its gentle Lord knew best.

Before that sweet humility,
The pride of man rebuked lay dead,
Before a faith that questioned not,
Proud reason bowed its haughty head.

O heart of mine remember now,
None but a child can do His will,
Naught but a faith that questions not,
Can win His sweet approval still.

For none will enter Heaven's gate,
And none will join the undefiled,
And none will sing the glad new song,
Except he be a little child.

My mom and dad and Grandma Jennie all came from Minnesota. Complete silence reigned as people filed out after the funeral service and waited for the hearse to start the procession to the cemetery. I appreciated the silence.

Erlice Dykstra was Alex Morrison's secretary. We knew Erlice well and Fred suggested she invite Alex to the funeral. He came, both to the funeral and the cemetery.

The state highway patrolman who investigated the accident told us it was an unavoidable accident. Noble Larue, one of the most trusted men in the county, told Fred that Alex was drunk, and others said they had seen him in the bar. Money would not have brought our little girl to life again, and we didn't even consider bringing Alex to court. It's possible the accident served as an impetus for Alex to stop drinking.

All the pall bearers were old people who were special to Sue: Vern Hamilton, Paul Stipe, Fred Kammerer (Susie's husband) and Wes Coleman. Sue used to come out to the clinic, and anybody of the grandparent vintage sitting there would soon find a small girl sitting on their lap. After her death we received cards from many people we hardly knew, people who remembered the little girl who sat on their laps, quietly enjoying the attention.

We learned a few things from this experience. For one, we now understand that the people who can give the most comfort are the people who have had a similar experience. Another thing we know is that, when you go to offer condolences and there are small children in the family, it is thoughtful to bring a coloring book or a small toy for the kids. Also, it is a fact that we, and maybe most people who have been bereaved, want to talk about the one they have buried.

***

Then came the nightmares. I would wake and sit in the living room. Because of the yard light shining through the sliding glass door, I could indistinctly see the brown sofa to my left, the old trunk under the large framed picture on the wall in front of me, and feel the warm carpet under my feet.

Our life style had changed since Sue's birth, but now there was a different dimension, an understanding about life we hadn't known. I struggled with guilt, thinking of all the "what if's" and "why didn't I's" a person thinks of after a tragedy.

Why didn't I go with Jill? Why didn't I at least go upstairs and watch out the window? I could have stopped the little girls with only a word, and gone out to help Jill with the package. Why did I even think it necessary to teach Jill about traffic? Why didn't I wait until school started and walk to the bus with her? Such were my thoughts, as I sat so many nights, sleepless.

In later years Jill admitted nightmares about Sue's death plagued her also. We haven't talked much about it with Kay. They were both so young, just babies really, and when I look back and realize I was only 27, it's a wonder we didn't have a worse time than we did. How did we know how to cope?

Our baby, Joel, was two when Sue, three-and-a-half, was killed on July 8, 1968. We have a hymn that says, "In love the Father ever veils the future." God protects us by not showing us coming disasters. How devastating it would have been if we had known at this time that Joel's physical slowness foretold a wheelchair in our living room—a wheelchair and later a blue granite gravestone alongside Sue's pink one. It is good we do not know the future.

DIAGNOSIS

People ask, "When did you first notice a problem with Joel?"
Our realization there was a problem came slowly. We noticed
he'd put his head down on the floor as he crawled, but it looked
as though he simply wanted to be on the same level as the toy
car he pushed. Later we commented to each other that his calf
muscles bulged more than the girls' but that didn't worry us.

Didn't most boys have different looking leg muscles than girls?

I don't remember at what age Joel walked, but know Jill, Kay, and Sue walked earlier, and Jill, in particular, was slower than most children. It's when we saw how Joel stood up from the floor that alarm bells rang. He'd laboriously maneuver to position his feet under him, put his hands on his bent knees, and push himself straight with his arms. As he became more proficient with walking and started running, he looked like a child with a slight case of cerebral palsy, an awkward, slow gait.

Talking came slowly also, but that was mainly the fault of the family females. A smile, an indecipherable noise, a pointing finger, and we understood what the baby of the clan wanted or meant, and jumped to fulfill his every need. Why should he talk when he controlled us with a smile?

Dr. Campbell saw all our kids regularly, and Joel's physical abilities or lack thereof did not worry him. He labeled me, "an overly concerned mother," and dismissed my questions.

"Please, Dr. Campbell," I said during one office visit. "Joel's in kindergarten this year. If you'd go watch him play with the other kids you'd see what I'm talking about. Joel does not walk or run normally. What is wrong?" I knew if he'd watch Joel at school it would pique his interest. He promised to do this but didn't.

So we decided to try out the new doctor in town, in spite of his hippie appearance and his propensity to treat everyone with acupuncture. This pony-tailed young M.D. in jeans and a red flannel shirt, examined Joel, then sat down to consult with me. He didn't tell me in plain words that he thought Joel mentally deficient, but his body language and what he didn't say, clearly gave me that message.

His opinion, although I didn't agree with it, spurred me to make an appointment with the experts at the Child Development Center in Missoula. There the doctors agreed with the hippie.

They told me Joel ranked in the low end of normal intelligence, which they insisted caused his physical problems. We disagreed with these experts, knowing they had failed to get him to communicate. Joel's intelligence showed in many different ways, so that didn't concern us. His physical disability did.

Fred's knees decided they were overworked and started bothering him enough that he made an appointment with an orthopedist in Missoula, who agreed to exam Joel at the same time. All the previous doctors had shown no real interest in a diagnosis. This orthopedist understood our questions, and he wanted an answer for us.

The others examined Joel while he sat on their exam table, but the procedure with the orthopedist differed. He asked Joel to pull off his shirt, unbuckle his belt, and remove his jeans, and he waited and watched while Joel followed instructions.

After Joel re-dressed himself, the next thing the doctor asked was for him to run down the hall, which Joel obediently did, to the best of his ability. This the doctor watched with particular interest, and during the consultation with Fred he told him, "It's a dirty word, but I think it may be muscular dystrophy. We'll run a plasma creatine phosphokinase (CPK) test, which is a blood test that measures deterioration of the muscles. It's used often when people have heart attacks."

Before Fred left Missoula that day he visited the library and researched muscular dystrophy, bringing material home for me to read. As I read, my insides plummeted and I felt shivery and sick. Joel's symptoms fit the picture of Duchenne muscular dystrophy to a tee. When I looked at our son, it was impossible to grasp he might have a disease with no cure and a life expectancy in the late teens.

Then the test results came back. Negative. Joel did not have muscular dystrophy, which was news that should have elated us, except we couldn't quite make ourselves believe the negative results. The information Fred unearthed in the library answered all the questions we had asked ourselves, all the "why's" that had plagued us.

It brought us back to square one. Now what? If not muscular dystrophy, what was wrong? Was it something that could be corrected if caught early? Were the Child Development Center doctors right and low intelligence the problem?

A few weeks in Selma Sederstrom's first grade class, and words and sentences and paragraphs spewed forth from our son. Mrs. Sederstrom bragged about his abilities. The questions continued to come. The blood test said Joel did not have muscular dystrophy. Joel's school progress disproved the low intelligence theory. Could we just ignore the fact our son did not walk or run easily? We always came back to the results of the literature search Fred did at the library, and knew we must positively rule out muscular dystrophy.

Contacting the Muscular Dystrophy Association was the next step. They made an appointment for Joel at the Seattle Children's Hospital. I don't remember how long we waited for the appointment, but do recall the thoughts that whirled through my head as I looked at our son. *Find out what's wrong. Hurry up. Do something. Now.*

The appointment information finally landed in our mailbox. Joel and I would drive to Seattle while Fred, Jill and Kay stayed home to tend to the business. Even at nine and ten years of age, the girls' chores helped the clinic operation. I packed a suitcase, wrote down directions to Seattle and to the hospital, and Joel and I took off.

Today I would think a drive of less than 500 miles a simple affair. However, the longest distance I had driven by myself before this was the 85 miles to Missoula. The mountains through the narrow part of Idaho did not bother me, the traffic around Spokane I took in stride. After Spokane it was smooth going, except for the niggling worry in my mind about Seattle. Would I know what lane to be in for my exit? How fast would the traffic be? What if I got lost?

Joel chattered and played in the back seat, oblivious to my fears. Then we hit the Seattle traffic on 1-5.

"Hush, Joel. I need to concentrate," I told him. "Mom's not used to this traffic."

He glued his little nose to the window, watching, while my knuckles glued themselves to the steering wheel. I took time to count the lanes of traffic, six lanes. Was it really six lanes or did I count wrong? I moved over another lane and saw my exit sign ahead—NE 45th Street, Sand Point Way. "We're almost there, Joel,"

"Almost where?"

"Almost to the hospital where they're going to check you over."

As he thought about this, we drove up to a huge edifice. The words, Seattle Children's Hospital emblazoned on the front, informed me it was the right place, and a sign pointed to a parking deck. I parked, got out our suitcase and released my captive son. Suitcase in one hand, Joel clutching the other, I entered the hospital. The space, the people scurrying around, the figures lounging here and there, obviously waiting for someone or something, even the smell of sickness, disinfectant and sweat, all increased my anxiety.

Joel tugged at my hand and I looked down. His entire being seemed stiff, both eyes and all senses on full alert. I smiled at him, I hoped encouragingly, and found our way to the information desk. To my relief, a member of the staff took over, taking us on a quick tour of the part of the hospital we would be in, finally depositing us, and much written information, in our assigned room. There we would spend the next days and nights. We'd stay until they found out why this small person with me could not run properly.

"Here's your son back," said the red-headed nurse who had taken Joel for his first appointment. "He behaved admirably. We put electrodes all over him, told him to lie still and not make a peep, and that's exactly what he did."

She looked down and grinned at my son and he looked up at her, pride shining in his eyes. Joel came to me and took my hand.

"I knew he'd be good."

When the nurse had arrived at our door that morning to get Joel, she had kindly and firmly told me to stay put, that kids always did better without their parents around. I knew it wouldn't matter with Joel, he'd behave the same way regardless, but I didn't argue. It gave me time to read all the info the admittance people had given me.

The next appointment was a quick and simple one; the doctors had ordered a CPK test and Joel gave his blood without a murmur. This time the lab results came back a resounding positive. In fact, Joel tested four times higher than most boys with Duchenne, and the doctor who talked to me said he considered the results from the former test a lab error.

Now we knew the worst, and, in a odd way, the results relieved us. At least we hadn't missed some obscure disease with an easy cure, a disease which would now be incurable because we waited too long.

***

After the psychiatrist put Joel through her hoops, she called me in for a conference. She rose from behind her desk, a tall, thin woman who I thought probably was in her fifties, but looked young and vibrant.

"It's been a pleasure to work with your son," were her first words as she shook my hand.

She sat down behind her desk as she waved me to a seat. Her smile made a bright spot in the gray Seattle day.

"I can tell you good news," she said. "Joel's I.Q. tested very high. But you will likely have some problems with his education. The administrators of schools love to dump the physically handicapped in special education classes. Never, and I mean never, let them do that."

She stressed, "You'll have to fight for him. Be ruthless. Fight hard. This child, in particular, needs to be in regular classes." She leaned over her desk and said with fervor. "Some people ignore the education of their dystrophic children with the attitude, 'Why bother, they won't live long.' But who knows? If the researchers find a cure, then those children will be cured but completely uneducated."

***

I'm hazy on the time Joel and I stayed at the hospital. It seemed a long time, but maybe was only a week. They put him through all kinds of tests, even though they knew the diagnosis. Research hospitals focus on causes of disease. After an exhaustive study the doctors decided that, in our case, a spontaneous gene mutation occurred between Joel and myself, not an uncommon situation.

Normally a mother passes the gene down to her son, and daughters of that mother can be carriers without showing symptoms of Duchenne. Girls can get other kinds of muscular dystrophy, but not Duchenne. They didn't think our girls would be carriers, but the doctors suggested we take them to Spokane, Washington once a year, while they were still young, to get them checked. Spokane had the closest muscular dystrophy clinic.

The diagnosis made, the research finished, Joel and I left for home—a drive that seemed endless. Though I tried to be cheerful, Joel wasn't fooled, and his happy chattering ceased. We stopped at a diner for lunch, and after he ate his fill, my young son got off his chair and walked up and down the aisle while I finished my coffee. The few people eating in there greeted him. I supposed they wondered why he walked like he did, as he already walked with his stomach protruding. It was the way he kept his balance.

That's the best it will get, I felt like telling them. He'll never get any better.

THREE MOTHERS

Misery doesn't always love company. Sometimes you want to feel special in your pain, want to relish your self-pity. You don't want anyone "one-upping" your troubles by whispering their problems in your ear.

We three young women understood that, as we silently sat, burrowed in soft sofas, Coke or coffee at our elbows, the only light the flickering, muted, television set. For days we had waited together, watching the Seattle grayness seep through the windows while doctors examined our children. At night we slept in narrow cots by their high, white cribs.

When we talked, it was of mundane matters; the tasteless cafeteria food, a cheerful nurse, the abundance of children's toys available in the lounge where we waited. Each of us knew the outlines of the others' problems, but we did not intrude, did not ask questions that might shatter control, or that might reduce our own self-pity. We sat together, but our minds were focused on our individual children.

An open door led to a wide hallway, through which wafted a pungent odor of disinfectant and alcohol. The hospital smells and sounds were background, contributing to the feeling of time suspended. Life went on outside the building, but we were not part of it.

I thought I wanted to recapture reality one evening, so after Joel fell asleep I went for a walk. The soft, misty rain collected on and slipped off my face, while forced thoughts of home, family and everyday chores slipped through my mind. I held onto nothing, but seemed determined to feel like a tragic figure in an English novel, tramping through the wet moors with my melancholy thoughts. Finally, ashamed of feeling sorry for myself, I went inside to join the others.

I brushed my damp hair back and sighed. Pam glanced at me, shifting her weight on the soft cushions as she crossed and uncrossed her legs. Pam was a blonde, whose white dress caught and reflected the television's varying colors. "I'm sorry I got so mad this afternoon," she said.

"It's okay. I understand."

Her daughter had cancer. The mother had guilt. That morning the dietitian lectured Pam, insisting the child should eat only healthy foods. After lunch, Pam told me, "I've tried everything. All she wants is french fries and ketchup. I can't force her to eat, and I hate to hear her cry."

Pam had shown her frustration that afternoon when Joel, with a giggle, tried to hitch a ride on her daughter's trike. The trike started to tip as Pam and I watched, aghast. Joel jumped off when it began to lean, but the damage was done. The small, weak girl desperately hung onto the trike's handlebars as she felt herself going. Trike and girl fell in a heap, her bald head hitting the hard floor with a thump.

It happened slowly, but not so slowly that either of us could save her. Joel's giggles stopped abruptly. His brown eyes widened in surprise. I watched, my mouth open in shock, as Pam examined her daughter for bumps and blood. There were none, nothing but bitter tears and shaking sobs.

"Why don't you watch him?" Pam yelled at me. "He's a little brat. Don't let him near her again."

Joel was a sensitive, quiet boy, and I wanted to defend him but couldn't. To hurt that fragile child seemed monstrous. He didn't mean to, I wanted to say. It was true but inadequate. And if I said anything I would cry. I never cried in front of Joel.

When Pam apologized, and I told her I understood, I meant it. I understood guilt. I understood frustration. A doctor had grilled me that day, repeatedly going over everything I ate during my pregnancy, any pills or drugs I took, any stress I experienced. Like a lawyer, he asked a question, then ten minutes later asked the same question in a different way, not satisfied with my answer. It felt like he was trying to catch me in a lie, like he thought I was withholding some vital information that would tell him why there had been a gene mutation causing our son to have muscular dystrophy.

Marge, the third mother, tossed her dark hair back, stirred and stretched when she heard Pam apologize. She knew why her baby was slow. A high fever caused convulsions, convulsions caused loss of oxygen to the brain, loss of oxygen caused brain damage. How much damage? That was the answer she wanted. Then she could go home and deal with it. Flicking cigarette ashes into an overflowing ashtray she sat up and looked at us.

"I want . . ." she said, but a racket at the door interrupted her.

With a clatter of keys, the janitor walked in, clumsily bumping his ladder on the door casing. He squinted his eyes, swept back his long, greasy hair, nodded in our direction, and said, "Sorry to interrupt, ladies. Need to fix this light."

Carefully he unfolded and set up the wooden ladder, made sure it locked in place, and then, setting each dirty shoe carefully, one rung at a time, he slowly climbed up. Three pairs of eyes turned to watch his progress. When he reached to unscrew the light bulb, the action exposed a flabby, white, hairy belly between his blue tee shirt and worn jeans. Holding the burnt out bulb in one hand, he pulled a good one out of his pocket, again gave us a view of his belly as he screwed that one in, then, with one hand clutching the old bulb, laboriously descended. Three young women sat quietly while he folded the ladder up, hoisted it under his arm and left, again hitting the door casing.

After he disappeared, Marge finished. "I want to go home. I miss my husband. I'm so horny even the janitor is beginning to look good." Our subdued laughter sounded loud in the late night stillness.

We would all go home soon. Reality would slap us when we got out of this soft, dark cocoon; the reality of burying a child before adulthood, the reality of raising a not-perfect child in a world that demands perfection, the reality, for me, of watching my son gradually die. Reality would force me to hold back tears, be cheerful in front of an intelligent child who knew what he could do this year he wouldn't be able to do the next year.

There was no more conversation that evening. As we went to our cots, I mulled over this; no matter how badly someone else hurts, their pain does not diminish my pain, nor does my hurt alleviate theirs. Maybe tomorrow I'll be able to share more with the others.

CHRISTMAS PROGRAM

In first grade Jill decided she didn't want to attend her first school Christmas program, so she simply didn't tell us about it. We didn't have to worry about it happening again. Her younger sister could be counted on to inform us of all school activities.

Accordingly, the first school Christmas program we attended was during Kay's first year of school. On this momentous night I fussed over both my girls, putting pretty dresses on them and doing their hair in neat pony tails. Kay wore a pink dress with pink ribbons in her hair, Jill an orange, patterned favorite and orange ribbons. In keeping with the season, winter decided we needed a taste of snow, so I dug our overshoes out of the closet.

"My overshoes are dirty, Mommy," Kay complained.

I checked the clock. "Time to go. We don't have time to clean them. Here's your coat," and I hustled them out the door.

As we entered the school's double doors, I told the girls.

"Don't forget to take off your overshoes when you get to your classrooms."

"I won't forget, Mommy," they answered in tandem, and they turned to go to their classrooms while Fred, Joel and I headed for the auditorium.

Rows of folding chairs lined up before the stage. Considering the entire town only had about 600 souls living in it, and the area surrounding town was sparsely populated, there was a good crowd of people sitting in those chairs. Most everyone looked familiar. I chuckled to myself when I realized I probably knew the names of all their family pets better than I knew their kids' names. I, however, did know the name of the youngster who sat with the family just ahead of us.

When Joel started his pre-kindergarten class, even though he seldom talked, he came home and told me about this little boy in school and all the fun they had with one another. One evening I asked the little boy's name. He looked at me incredulously. Surely his mother knew the name of the boy he played with every day.

"You know, Mom," he said, disgust in his voice, "That little boy named Janet."

The girl who sat waiting for her sister to appear on the stage, was named Janet White. Of that I was certain. She had close-cropped hair, and looking over her shoulder, I saw she was wearing jeans, Christmas or not.

An extremely tall, decorated Christmas tree stood in one corner of the auditorium, a few poinsettia plants on the floor in front of the stage. Nothing was elaborate, but the total effect was Christmasy and would have been fun had I not been so nervous.

I fidgeted, ridiculously anxious about my young daughters simply standing in a group and singing a couple of Christmas carols. What could possibly go wrong? Mothers feel things keenly when it comes to their offspring, hurting when they hurt, rejoicing when they rejoice, and blushing when they are embarrassed.

Joel sat on the aisle seat. He leaned over, looked back down the aisle, than glanced at me, his brown eyes signaling, "Here they come." Kay and her classmates marched in and took their places, Kay in the front row. Her hair was still neat, her pink dress unwrinkled and clean, but her red, mud-spattered overshoes glistened wetly in the overhead lights! Our daughter stood straight and tall, found where we sat and broke into a big smile.

I relaxed. Yes, she had forgotten to take off her overshoes, but it wasn't bothering her and it wasn't going to bother her mother either.

RAISING JOEL

A visit to or from any of the Dykstras, particularly Al Dykstra, delighted Joel, who used those visits to replenish his supply of jokes and stories. He listened wide-eyed as Al held court, and for days afterward he'd pop up with, "Remember Al's story about the skunk?" Or, "Remember that joke about the boat and the fisherman? Remember? Al told it." His eyes shone, as laughter burst out.

Jokes and stories didn't constitute all our youngest child's repertoire, he being an expert on ways to annoy his sisters. They, in turn, treated him like the exasperating little brother he sometimes was.

While working in the kitchen one summer day, I heard Jill say, satisfaction and exasperation both ringing in her voice, "There. Now you'll stay out of our hair."

Screams and yells came from an indignant Joel. Jill knew he could no longer get up without help and, tired of his pestering, had dragged him into the living room and deposited him squarely in the middle. He was stuck–his voice his only weapon.

Both girls spent time with Joel, but Jill and Joel were less simpatico in their play than were Kay and Joel. Those two used the basement as their playground, and if you didn't understand what you looked at when you went down there, you'd think, "What a mess." Wooden blocks of all shapes and sizes covered the floor, along with cars, Play Skool people, a house and a service garage. They built an elaborate set up, spending hours arranging and re-arranging towns, roads, parking lots and homes for all the people.

It amused me when I, without looking, could tell that Jill's ever present book had been put aside and she'd gone to see what Kay and Joel were up to. The noise level rose considerably.

"No, Jill, that's a house for Joel's people," I heard Kay say.

"Hey, that doesn't go there!" Joel raised his voice in protest.

Jill didn't want to play, she enjoyed creating a little havoc in a quiet day.

***

The only thing to do for Joel was to keep his mind and body active. We went to physical therapists and did therapy at home; otherwise, we tried to raise him like we did our healthy girls. A visit to an unknown woman showed me how important the latter was.

Someone, I don't know who, brought my attention to a newspaper article about a family in Polson who had two boys with Duchenne muscular dystrophy. The article said the parents were taking the boys to a Colorado medical center for a treatment involving gold.

Any information about treatment raised skepticism in both Fred and I, having been inundated with many types of harebrained "cures" from any number of people. However, we decided it wouldn't hurt if I went to see the mother. Even if the treatments weren't doing any good, it might be helpful to see how they coped. It couldn't be easy.

I called, and the mother, Nancy, sounded eager to meet me and talk about her boys. Thus started an afternoon which gave me a soapbox subject that has lasted my entire life.

As I rang the doorbell of the house, a white, ranch style, I looked around the yard. It was neat, the grass newly mowed. Nancy opened the door and greeted me with a pleasant smile, indicating I should come in. She wore blue jeans, a red sweatshirt and had her blonde hair tied back in a pony tail—a nice looking young woman.

When I followed her into the tidy living room, the smell of urine hung in the air and I involuntarily looked around to find the source. Two boys sat on scatter rugs in the middle of the floor, obviously unable to move off the rugs. The smell emanated from them, I felt certain. Had their muscles deteriorated enough they couldn't control their urine? Is that going to happen to Joel? I wondered. Nancy and I introduced ourselves, she introduced William and Casey, and we sat down. I explained I called her because I wanted to meet someone who was experiencing problems we also were facing, or were going to have to face as Joel grew older. With a gesture at her sons, the young woman started talking.

"These boys are always up to something. One day William wanted to get in the boat in the back yard, so I lifted both William and Casey into the boat, not knowing they had matches in their pockets. Isn't it something how boys love to play with matches?

"Luckily the kitchen window was open, because it wasn't long and I heard them yelling. I looked out and saw the boat in flames, so ran out, grabbed the boys and hauled them out. They had set some rags on fire, and canvas in the front of the boat had started on fire also. If I hadn't heard them, they could have burnt up with the boat."

"That was scary. You have another son, right? One who doesn't have muscular dystrophy? Was he in the boat also?"

"No, our youngest doesn't have it, but he was in school."

"William and Casey don't go to school?"

"No, I try to teach them here at home. But they're always misbehaving. I can't get them to pay attention."

During our conversation the two boys had been listening, wiggling their rugs around and giggling over their misadventures.

I changed the subject and asked about the gold treatment. She hesitated before answering, but then admitted they hadn't seen any change.

"It's very expensive," she told me, "they're on an experimental program though, so all we have to pay for is the trip."

When I asked her the next question, I already knew the answer. The newspaper reporter had asked it himself. "Have any others in your family had Duchenne?"

"Oh, yes. My mother's brothers both had it, and one of my brothers died of it also. We're so happy we have a healthy son. I'm what they call a carrier, you know."

Why, I wanted to ask, as I bit my tongue, why, when you knew exactly how bad this disease was, did you go ahead and have three boys? Surely the doctors would have checked and known the first one had muscular dystrophy before you got pregnant with the second—two children doomed to be prisoners in their own bodies, two children who faced a short but hard life, just so you and your husband could have one healthy boy. There could easily have been three boys sitting on rugs in the living room.

My head started aching, and I knew I couldn't stay there without spouting off, so after a few more minutes I excused myself and left.

No one was along to listen to me on the drive home, which was a blessing, as I alternated between ranting and raving and bawling. Why? Why when she knew she was a carrier of a terrible disease, would she blithely have one boy after another, hoping to get one healthy one? Like having throwaway kids. Was that humane? And she let those boys sit on their rugs doing nothing, expected nothing of them, could not get them to even listen when she tried to teach them. Why didn't she send them to school? Even a special ed class would be much, much better than nothing. I vowed to try my best to help Joel live as normal a life as possible.

When my writing group read my account of the woman with the two boys with Duchenne Muscular Dystrophy (DMD), they had questions and comments that deserve to be addressed. I reminded them I wrote this memoir telling only what our family had observed, and with the knowledge available 40 years ago.

Q. Did Joel have a problem controlling his urine?

A. No, Joel did not have a problem. DMD does not affect the smooth muscles, such as the bladder and bowels. William and Casey's problem was likely a behavior problem

Q. How did the boys get matches when they couldn't get around?

A. I don't know, but back then, when so many people smoked, most homes had matches and ashtrays available.

Q. Why, if they wanted a boy so much, didn't they adopt?

A. Again, I don't have the answer. You do have to remember that adoption is not easy and it is expensive–those may have been factors. I hear people say, "I don't want to adopt. It's hard telling what disease or problem you will get when you adopt." That's true, but in the case of William and Casey's parents, they knew the chance of having a son with DMD was 50%. And the chance of having a daughter who was a carrier was also 50%.

Q. Is the disease painful?

A. No.

Q. What did William and Casey's parents believe about abortion?

A. The subject did not came up when I visited. At that time, doctors suggested aborting the males if you were a known carrier. Now, of course, with advances in medicine they can test and determine if your unborn child has some of the mutations causing DMD.

Q. Did you think the boys were of normal intelligence?

A. About 1/3 of the boys with DMD have learning disabilities. At the time I visited, I never thought the boys lacked in intelligence, I personally blamed the way they were being raised. However, I was not there for very long.

***

Joel's classmates in Hot Springs helped Joel feel as normal as possible. They treated Joel like they did one another–laughed with him, helped him and teased him. When he fell down, they picked him up, dusted him off, and sent him on his way again. Like all boys do to one another, they made fun of him, but no one made fun of his physical disability. Not for long anyway.

Jolene Jacobson stopped by and said to me, "I hear your son was the reason for a fight at school."

"Joel? What did he do?"

"Joel didn't do anything. Randy Baxter did. A new kid came to school, Ryan somebody. He called Joel some name that Randy took offense at. So Randy took him behind the school at recess and cleaned his clock."

"Well, I wonder what will happen now."

"I don't think the kid will try it again."

Ryan didn't try it again. When he got to know Joel better, the two became good friends. Joel's sisters and his friends helped give him a normal boyhood.

***

During recess, when he was a fifth grader, Joel kicked a soccer ball, fell and twisted his leg. The school principal called me and I dropped everything, drove to the school and took the injured boy home. Fred set his son up on the examining table and palpated the leg. "It's broken," he diagnosed.

A visit to Dr. Campbell filled my afternoon, and Joel came home with his leg in a white cast. Joel started getting acquainted with his "wheels," the wheelchair which waited in our living room. We hoped this was not an ominous omen for the future, but would be temporary.

After Dr. Campbell took the cast off, physical therapy became even more important. An older man in town did massage and owned a whirlpool tub. His place of business filled one of the cabins which constituted the bulk of our town of Hot Springs. I took Joel there regularly for a soak in the whirlpool, and after his leg warmed in the hot, swirling water, we exercised and stretched it.

Anxious to get Joel out of the wheelchair, I told him one day, "Let's try out your leg. I'll help you as you walk down the hall."

He put one hand on the wall, which is the way he walked before the break, and I took the other arm to steady him. He couldn't do it. His legs buckled, and he started to fall. That night, when I put him to bed, tears came into his brown eyes and he said, "I don't think I'll ever walk again." It was the first and last time I saw him cry over his situation. The prognosis of a ten-year-old proved correct.

***

One night I was stuffing Joel's legs into his pajamas when he blurted out. "Ryan and Randy have the best time so far."

"What do you mean, Joel"

"Oh, you know, Mom. Bathroom time."

"No, I don't know."

"The boys are supposed to help me to the toilet. They take turns, two of them wheel me in there, help me drop my pants and lift me on the toilet. The other two stay in the classroom and time them. So far Randy and Ryan have the best time."

"I see."

Not long after I smiled over this interesting information, the school principal called me.

"Randy and Joel had an accident with Joel's wheelchair. Joel's okay, but we'd like you to take him home." Rushing to the school, I found Randy Baxter and Joel in the principal's

121

office. Both looked close to tears.

"I didn't mean to hurt him," said Randy. "We've done it many times and never had trouble."

"I'm not hurt and I don't want to go home," Joel said, emphatically.

I pieced together what happened. Their school sat at the top of a small hill, and during recess, early in the school year, the boys discovered the hill made an exciting ride. Randy pushed Joel to the top, gave the wheelchair a push, and jumped on the back. Joel, the driver, steered with his brake extensions, keeping the wheelchair on the sidewalk. By the time they got to the bottom, the wheelchair and boys went at a good clip, a thrilling enough ride they did it often. However, the inevitable happened, and this particular day the wheelchair hit a crack or a hole and upset. Joel's head hit the sidewalk, and the blow knocked him out.

The principal thought Randy should be punished. I demurred.

"Why should Randy be punished any more than Joel? I'm sure they've learned their lesson."

Later I explained to him how much it meant to us that the boys made Joel feel like one of them. He punished no one, and the boys did not (at least to my knowledge) try the fast ride down the sidewalk again.

***

Ryan pushing Joel's cart

A wheelchair works fine on hard surfaces, but is difficult to move on sand, soft dirt, or through the sagebrush so common in our little spot of Montana. Joel's friends wanted to be outside playing when they came to our house, and pushed and shoved his wheelchair around.

Fred found a machinist who made a cart with large bicycle wheels, one that could be either pushed by a friend or pulled behind a bike. The cart looked clumsy, but made it possible for the boys to push Joel through the pasture and around the yard.

Kay and Jill pulled the cart behind their bikes, but it was tough going for even those muscular, though slim, girls. Bored with home one summer day, Jill hooked the cart behind her bike and Jill, Kay, and Joel all went to town.

Apparently everything went fine until Jill forgot her trailer and turned a corner too sharp. The cart's wheel went up on the curb, and Joel and the cart ended up on their sides in the street. Her passenger, well buckled in, sustained no injury, but Jill felt terrible. Neither of the girls pulled Joel around behind their bikes much after that accident.

* * *

We put Joel's life in danger every time we visited his cousins, the Eckels, on their farm. The cousins, six blond, blue-eyed boys, with one girl thrown in for good measure— all healthy, vigorous and loud—gave both Joel and his cart a workout during these visits. I have no idea where all they took him.

My sister called me to the window one day, just in time to see one of her sons give Joel a huge boost onto the roof of the hen house. As he sat there with a big grin on his face, we just stayed in the house and let the kids have their fun.

A mechanized gizmo made from a car chassis, which the Eckel kids called the putt-putt, figured high on these farm visits. The steering wheel was in front, rough board seats occupied the middle, a Briggs and Stratton motor putt-putted along at the rear. One of the cousins, or maybe it was the group, discovered that Joel's cart pulled nicely behind the putt-putt. At least it pulled nicely until they got going too fast or hit a bump and the cart and rider tipped over.

"He'd be covered in road dust," my nephew, Jay, told me recently, "But he always wanted to do it again. He dared us to do most anything with him, such as climbing up to the tree house. We'd lift him to the first rung on the ladder, and he'd hang on until one of us pushed from behind and he could make the next rung. A little chancy but we were careful."

Careful might not be the right word, but if Joel sustained any scratches or bruises at the farm they've been long forgotten.

GIRLS AND ATHLETICS

Jill and Kay never said much about the day-to-day happenings in school, but we were privy to some extra-curricular activities. For Jill these consisted mainly of sports. When still in Montana, she spent her recess playing ball with the boys, while Kay sat on the front steps talking, or playing with the girls.

Basketball, track, and cross country all found their way onto Jill's schedule, and she worked hard at her play. When watching Jill run, stretching those long legs so she looked low to the ground, I marveled at the stamina it took. I marveled also at the groceries consumed.

Either Kay's lack of a competitive spirit or just not being interested held her back, yet we felt she was a natural athlete. She sat a horse like an expert from the git go, and we expected her to take to riding like the proverbial duck to water. Occasionally riding with Jill sparked her interest, but that was enough. Our praise made no difference. It slid off her just as easily as she could slip off a horse.

Every summer someone gave swimming lessons at the Hot Springs' bathhouse pool, and I sent the two girls to town on their bikes. I needed to let them go, but the first few times whenever they'd get out of sight, I'd pace the floor and cry until I got control of myself. They rode on the horse path close to the fence line, not on the highway, but it still made me afraid.

The day the girls had their swimming test, I asked Mae

Hamilton to come and answer the phone so I could go to the pool to check on how they were doing. Not a proficient swimmer myself, I had, however, suffered through enough lessons to know what to look for. What I saw amazed me. Jill did well, though swimming wasn't her favorite activity, but Kay's form was great, and she made it all look so easy. Other than for lessons, however, neither girl spent much time in the pool.

Kay never tried very hard at running either. Before they grew old enough to think chasing one another around the yard was kid stuff, I watched Jill chase Kay, with Jill outrunning her every time. Except when Kay's ire rose. Then, with just a small spurt of speed, she'd quickly catch Jill.

When we moved to Fargo, North Dakota, Jill was 15, Kay 14. Either the first or second fall, Jill coerced her sister into joining the newly formed cross-country team. After one meet she came home steaming. "If Kay tried," she said, "she could beat all of us. She finishes the race and isn't even puffing."

"My muscles get tired," replied Kay.

One girl impressed us with her athletic ability, even though she wasn't interested, the other with the effort she expended.

September 22, 1972

Good Afternoon to Doris . . .

It's a beautiful fall day here in Montana, and outside beckons. However, I'm stuck with the phone, so while it's quiet, I'll start a letter to you.

Butterscotch barked this morning, and when I looked out, sure enough, a colorful, graffiti-painted van drove up, full of hippies. That dog never barks at anyone except hippies. Even if they aren't in a "hippie van" she recognizes them immediately when they get out of whatever vehicle they're in. She's too well-mannered to growl, but looks like she'd like to.

I'm not too fond of them either. A bunch camp in Lolo National Forest and come in with their barefoot, snotty-nosed kids, who definitely look malnourished. It puts a damper on an otherwise nice day. California must have too many of the long-haired peaceniks, so they are starting to disperse. Us local yokels hope a Montana winter chases them back home. They don't fit in well here with the cowboys and Indians.

Fred had to leave for a few days for a veterinary thing, so I brought the old sewing machine cabinet downstairs and refinished it. I used a black stain like I did on the chest, and it turned out fine. Now I'll go find some white knobs for the drawers. "When the cat's away the mice will play."

My workload is considerably less when Fred's gone and the Ronan vets get all the work that can't wait.

How's the dairy business? And the kids?
Write again.

Georgia

WAYS TO TEASE A DOG

All the kids loved their pets. They gave them lots of attention, fed them, scolded them, cleaned up after them. Jill's favorites were the cat, Bugs, and the milk cow. Kay ended up with the dog, Butterscotch, as her special friend. Joel? I guess he saw them all as Equal Opportunity Friends. He liked the kittens, the gerbils and the hamster, the small animals, but Butterscotch occupied a large part in his heart also, particularly when he could still walk unassisted.

"Hey, Butterscotch. Want a ride?" Joel called. The golden retriever jumped into the red wagon. Grunting, the young boy picked the handle up from the ground and pulled the wagon slowly down the drive. "Butter, you're getting too big," he complained. "I need a ride. You should pull."

I smiled, as I watched and heard my son through the open kitchen window, but sorrow tiptoed through my being, ready to pounce at any time. Muscular dystrophy was slowing destroying Joel's muscles. Soon the dog-pulling game would make Joel's list of things, "I used to could do."

Whatever the kids did, it involved Butterscotch. She spent her puppyhood teasing them by pulling off their mittens and running, shaking her head, mittens dangling from her laughing face. In the spring we'd find mittens in the slush around the veterinary clinic and house, abandoned after Joel and the girls gave up and came in, hands as pink as the dog's lolling tongue.

Butterscotch matured, and the teasing switched from dog to boy. They played out a familiar scenario every morning and evening, making enough of a hubbub I could tell exactly what went on whether I was in the house or the adjoining clinic.

Joel's twice daily chore was to feed Butterscotch. The boy, brown eyes sparkling, delighted in taking her food from the kennel, where one of his sisters had prepared it, through the examining room. He'd pretend he was going to set it down by the clinic's back door.

"Butter, you want to eat? Well, come and get it. Nope, I won't set it down there, I think I'll go over this way."

Through the open area between the clinic's back door and the kitchen door, he'd go, food in hand.

"I'll set it here by the kitchen steps," he'd announce to the salivating animal, as she danced excitedly to the kitchen door. We had trained Butterscotch to stay within the imaginary line running from the kitchen door to the clinic's back door. Bouncing like Pooh's friend Roo, she'd follow the boy with her dinner from one door to the other.

"You think I'm going to let you have it this instant? Right now? Why should I let you have it so quick?

The dog, tail wagging, enjoyed the game and stayed

scrupulously behind the imaginary line keeping her out of the clinic proper and away from the clients with their pets. Finally, tiring, Joel set the food down. Butterscotch gulped her meal and licked the bowl clean.

"My, you're a pig. What do you mean, you want more? All gone, you silly."

Joel had playmates other than the dog. Kay and Jill spent time with him every day, as they enjoyed their vivacious little brother. Also, quite often when the school bus stopped at the road, one of Joel's school friends would jump off and come yelling Joel's name. His friends knew I picked Joel up and we always beat the bus home.

Sisters and friends, however, did not take up all the hours in a day, especially the summer hours. Many of those extra hours were spent with Butterscotch. I would find them out in the shed, the strawberry blonde coat of the dog blending with the boy's lighter hair, as they nosed through the latest batch of kittens. Or they would be in the pasture lying in wait for gophers, the dog's plumed tail moving rhythmically with anticipation.
Companions.

BUTCHER IT PAPA!

Fred decided to add a flock of sheep to the menagerie. His reasons were twofold; to bring in extra income and to give two girls more work. The sheep did not get to be a paying proposition, but the work situation intensified.

Since the girls were still pre-teens, the work started out as my responsibility. I watered the sheep, fed the sheep, and chased the sheep back into the pasture. They appreciated all I did for them so much that every one of them, whenever I stepped out the door, came running to the fence, bleating. Never valuing my fan club, I quickly decided the young girls were old enough, and thankfully transferred the work and the vociferous sheep to them.

Kay and Jill never seemed to mind the job. Fred castrated the lambs and docked their tails, leaving the day-to-day care to his daughters. Usually the first ewe to lamb in the spring surprised them, forcing them to herd the ewe and her lamb from the pasture to the shed.

After the first lambing they watched carefully and picked out the ones likely to lamb that night, bringing them into the shed before the event; to get a pregnant ewe in the shed was much easier than rounding up a lamb and its new mother. How they knew what to watch for I don't know and never asked. Jill's propensity leaned toward doing all work the easiest and most efficient way, and both girls kept their eyes open around animals, so it didn't surprise me. I doubt Fred ever complimented them on their accomplishment, but he often commented to me on their success rate.

Both of the girls understood the food chain part of the farming business. They enjoyed the lambs and loved to watch the lambs' endless games of tag and "King of the Hill," but when it came time to butcher, they helped Jim Andrews with the bloody job.

"Papa, a lamb broke her leg," they once greeted the veterinarian-in-residence. "Can you set it?"

Fred, working nearly around the clock with calving cows and scouring calves, did not want to take the time to splint the lamb's leg.

"Sure girls, I can set the leg. But, remember, after I get the cast on, you'll have to keep the lamb in the shed, clean the pen, water and feed it."

Neither of them hesitated. "Butcher it, Papa. Butcher it," they chimed, nearly in unison. Mr. Andrews butchered that lamb, and we ate it, no one regretting its untimely demise.

The youngsters learned how to work. My mother thought us too tough on them. She told me more than once that an hour's worth of chores before school was on par with child abuse. On a blustery, cold day I looked at the two sleeping girls and thought, maybe Mom's right. It wouldn't hurt me to feed and water the animals today. I even made the optimistic observation that the wind might die down by the time they left for school. So they slept peacefully for another hour and went cheerfully to school without doing the chores, probably wondering what ailed their mother.

The wind didn't die down, and it fought me, as I threw the hay bales around, wondering how those slightly built kids managed. It took me twice as long as it took them and I entered the house grouchy and tired. I never did it again.

SLAUGHTER

All of us frequently deplore man's cruelty to animals. When we hear of or see a horse, emaciated and swaying on its feet, a dog tied to a tree with no shelter, no water, no food, or cats wrestled into a burlap sack and drowned by those responsible for their care, our minds recoil.

Conversely, we seldom think or read about the innate cruelty between animals. In grade school, we learn about the animal kingdom's food chain, but later tend to forget or ignore the possible end to the cute little cottontail running across our lawn. Then we hear a screaming commotion in the night and find cottony balls hanging on the azaleas in the morning.

A rifle in our closet reminds me how nature's cruelty conflicts with people's sense of compassion. Fred bought the gun after dogs slaughtered our sheep, wanting to prepare himself in case it happened again.

We were gone that morning, but came home in the middle of the afternoon. It was a sunny, calm day. The light blue Montana sky stretched tightly from mountaintop to mountaintop over our valley. Rough greasewood bunched together along the fence, and yellow weed-flowers stood here and there in the grass. As we turned into our driveway, we noticed nothing wrong at first. Then we saw the sheep, running in all directions, bleating frantically.

"Oh no. Look. Dogs," said Fred, almost under his breath, each word outlined in disbelief.

Jumping from the pickup, my eyes searched the pasture, and I saw three, white, long-haired Samoyeds. One was chasing a sheep, the other two were eating a still-living ewe, snatching and pulling the innards which spilled from her belly. In their blood frenzy, the dogs ran furiously from sheep to sheep scattering blood and guts.

Fred hurried into the house. I stood, bile burning in my throat, watching the slaughter. Before we ever bought the sheep, Fred made great efforts to build a sturdy pasture fence by setting the posts deep in the hard clay and stretching woven wire taut. He then added electric fence to the outside, a couple feet from the ground, to shock any sheep-lusting dogs or coyotes. This fence kept the sheep safe only as long as the irrigation ditch was full of running water.

The ditch ran diagonally through the pasture and under the fence. When the ditch rider (the man responsible for the distribution of the irrigation water) turned the water off, the lack of water created a gap between the fence and the bottom of the ditch. Visible from the kitchen window, a dry ditch raised an imaginary red flag, and whoever was at home would dash out the door and block the gap with a piece of fencing. We had left home at the wrong time. Dogs had discovered the dry ditch and slipped through the opening.

Fred slammed the house door behind him. "I called Everett. He's coming over with his gun." Quietly we stood and watched the slaughter. I felt glad Kay and Jill weren't at home to see the carnage happening in their flock of twenty-five ewes..

Everett's dusty, red pickup came speeding down the road and into our driveway. He stopped, got out, reached back inside and picked his gun off the gun rack. No one said anything. Our eyes followed his denim-clad stride as he walked through the gate, adjusted his Stetson, aimed and fired. A dog flew up, then hit the ground with a thump, dead.

The shot woke the other dogs from their delirium, and they

abandoned their bloody feast. Up and down the fence they raced, searching for the gap. Everett shot again and another hesitated, then fell. Desperate, the third dog made a leap and flew over the fence. A white blur disappeared.

"Sorry I didn't get that one," Everett said as we joined him.

"Thanks, Everett," Fred said. "Guess I should get a gun."

All three of us stepped soberly through the flock, checking to see which ones were dead, which needed to be killed, and which could possibly be saved. Fred gathered supplies, first giving an overdose of anesthesia to the ones too mutilated to save, then he and I went to work.

We clipped the wool around the wounds, the sharp scissors crisply cutting the soft layers. The clean smell of disinfectant rose into the still air, as we poured it into open bellies, trusting it to do its job.

Fred left me to finish suturing surface wounds, as he had ranch calls he couldn't put off any longer. The menstrual smell of warm blood and the wet wool odor hung heavy as I leaned over the docile sheep, pulling catgut strands through skin and knotting them tightly. My tears mingled with the sheep's blood and I questioned; why, if the dogs were hungry, did they not just kill one sheep and eat it? Instead they made sport of killing as many as possible and done so in the most brutal way.

Dogs are carnivores and carnivores eat meat. We learn that in grade school when we learn about the food chain. What no one tells us is that carnivores also eat plants by eating the stomach and intestinal contents of herbivores. Does a cat delicately eat only the flesh of the mouse? No, a cat eats the entire mouse, bones, intestines and all. Dogs eat sheep the same way, first the intestines and intestinal ingesta, then the flesh.

A dead dog was lying near me, his jaws clenched on a piece of intestine, blood thickened on his face. I glared at it, stood up and kicked it viciously. "Why didn't you kill something your own size?" I screamed irrationally. "You big bully. Sheep of all things. You could've had your fun with something that could fight back." All this accomplished, of course, was making my toe hurt and my throat sore, but the outburst calmed me. I wiped my tears with my blood-sticky hand and went back to work.

SANTA CLAUS

Fred did not intend to add to the workload when he bought a Jersey heifer and bred her with semen from a Tarentaise bull, a popular exotic breed in the 1970's. He thought he'd sell her as a bred heifer and make a few dollars. His daughters changed that plan, as they fell in love with the gentle, brown and white heifer.

"Can we keep her Papa?" they questioned as they fondled her soft ears.

Their father looked them in their eyes. "If I let you keep that heifer," he declared, "the first time we have to tell you girls to milk her, she goes to market." He continued, "She'll need milking every morning and every night. Without fail."

"Yes, Papa. We will Papa."

And they did. I didn't know much about milking cows, but any picture in my mind consisted of a single milkmaid sitting on a stool on one side of the cow. Our girls took two stools, and one sat on each side. Apparently the heifer hadn't seen the same pictures I'd seen and didn't have preconceived notions, as she let them tie her up most anywhere and placidly chewed her cud while they got on with the job. More than once, after seeing the heifer tied up to a fence post being milked by the two girls, ranchers came chuckling into the clinic. "Never saw the like," they'd say, and shake their heads.

That heifer had my number, and with her offbeat sense of humor, pestered me continuously. Because of the dry climate, our small pasture needed water. A pump pumped water out of the irrigation ditch into pipes with sprinkler heads. Often the job of setting up the irrigation pipe in the pasture ended up on my to-do list, as everyone else conveniently disappeared to school or on a call.

The heifer stood patiently on the sidelines, waiting with her eyes wide open and her head cocked while I hooked each pipe together and set it in position, a straight line down the pasture. Finished, I'd check the pasture to see where the mischievous bovine was, and I swear she'd drop her head and innocently chomp on some grass, letting me know that she absolutely was not going to ruin my day. So, I'd run to start the pump.

Of course, the minute I'd turn my back, the little Jersey, in a blur of brown and white, would head for the pipe, knock one section down, and stand there smirking as she watched the pipe, like dominoes, slowly fall, one section at a time. I'd yell at her, and she'd run, tail in the air, happy for a little excitement in her day. If I'd been the swearing kind, I'd have given the ranchers competition.

Santa Claus was the moniker the girls gave her, which Fred and I considered an odd name, but it didn't take too long for even us slow learners to figure it out. Fred paid for the heifer, the semen he'd used to artificially inseminate her, and all the hay and feed. Our daughters sold all the extra milk and pocketed the money. They also claimed the money from the calf when it went to market. Pretty good deal for a couple pre-teens!

Nothing matched that milk in flavor. And the cream it produced, and the ice cream possible from that cream! It's a good thing we didn't count calories or cholesterol in those days and just enjoyed the bounty.

BUGS, THE CAT

An old man opened the clinic door. Under his left arm he held a struggling orange and white kitten, and in his left hand, a leash, at the end of which an overweight, light brown cocker spaniel resisted making an entrance. The gentleman sported tan dress pants, a navy blue sport jacket and a red and navy tie, a contrast to our usual jeans and cowboy shirt clad clientele.

As I hurried around the desk to help this natty looking stranger, he spoke rapidly. "This little cat needs his claws taken off. *All* his claws," he stated firmly. "And he needs castrating."

Lightly jerking the dog's leash, he continued. "This old boy, Buster, needs his glands cleaned again. He's scooting on his rear." Demonstrating, the cocker sat down, dragged his bottom a few feet, then looked up at his master. Opaque, cataract-dimmed eyes and a gray muzzle agreed with the adjective his owner used.

"Okay." I led the way into the kennel. "The kitten will have to stay overnight," I said while I spread newspapers in a cage.

We were proud of these new cages. Constructed of shiny stainless steel, they were easy to clean and disinfect. Sturdy doors and latches meant no more dogs tearing at wire or gnawing on wood to make their escape.

Unhooking the cat from the owner's shirt, I deposited him on the newspaper-padded cage floor and closed the door quickly. His large yellow eyes looked inquisitively around. "Ritt?" he questioned.

"What's the cat's name?" I asked.

"Bugs. He loves bugs–catches and eats all kinds. He's a nice cat, but my wife's an invalid with the thin skin us old folks are cursed with. When she pets him he turns over on his back and scratches her with the claws of all four paws. That's why I want all the claws removed."

By the time I recorded the animals' history, Fred arrived. I held the cocker while he donned latex gloves, lifted the stubby tail and inserted his finger, squeezing until the anal glands released their smelly load. We bid the old gentleman and his dog good-bye, Fred hurried off on his next call, and I settled back at the desk to finish figuring retail drug prices. Suddenly a small, furry ball thumped down right in the middle of the invoices.

"Riiiitt?" the ball trilled.

"How did you get out, kitty? Didn't I close the cage door? Back you go." I picked up and petted the kitten who promptly turned over and scratched my hands. Again, I put him in his cage and firmly latched the door. "Now you'll stay there," I informed him.

"Ritt?" he questioned again.

"No ritts about it," I answered. His big, solemn eyes followed me as I left the room.

Now more aware of kennel noises, I heard the cage latch rattling as I finished the last invoices. Soon all was quiet. I pushed back my chair to get up, and nearly ran over the orange and white kitten. "Bugs," I exclaimed. "How did you get out?" The cat followed me as I hurried into the kennel. The cage door hung wide open.

"Ritt," said Bugs, looking at me and then at the open cage door. "Riiiitt?"

"You are a gangly, big-eyed, no-good cat," I scolded. "And must be a relative of Houdini. I'll see how you manage this." Scooping the compliant cat into my arms, I put him into the

140

cage once again. After closing the door, I took a few steps to the side so Bugs couldn't see me. A thin leg reached out, curled around the latch and wiggled it. The cat leaned on the door as he wiggled the latch. Soon he had the cage open, and half fell, half jumped to the floor. Recovering himself, he looked around, saw me and said, "Ritt?"

"Ritt yourself young fellow." I went into the exam room, pulled out some adhesive tape, came back to my calm rebel and tossed him unceremoniously back into the cage. "That should do the trick," I told him as I taped the latch. "Don't teach your escape routine to anyone else." The phone rang and I went back to work.

At supper that night I told the story of the Houdini cat named Bugs. The kids barely swallowed their last bite before they ran out to investigate. Bugs, sedated after his castration and declawing ordeal, lay quietly, all four paws bandaged. He looked like one of the kittens with mittens in the old nursery rhyme.

"How come all four paws?" Jill asked, knowing that normally people only wanted the front two done. I explained the cat's propensity to scratch his invalid owner and also told them the origin of the name, Bugs.

Our client could not come after Bugs immediately, so we kept him in the cage for two days. Even with his bandaged paws, he would open the cage if it wasn't taped shut. This fascinated the kids. No other cat before, nor since for that matter, showed the intelligence required to open the cage doors. Bugs developed into a small celebrity.

When the owner came to collect the cat and pay the bill, I mentioned to him we all enjoyed his cat, helped them out the door, and promptly put them out of my mind.

***

"There are mice in the basement," Jill said, when we gathered for supper one evening.

"Yep. Lots of them," Kay agreed and made a face.

I was preoccupied, as I set the meal on the table and talked on the phone.

"Mice? You've seen them?" I said after I put down the phone.

"Yep. Lots of times," repeated Kay. "And we sleep down there."

"We'll have to set traps. Remind me to put mousetraps on my list."

Calving and its attendant problems kept us busy and I completely forgot about the mice. Either the girls made friends with the little rodents or decided their kindhearted mom wouldn't set mousetraps, as they didn't say anything more about mice.

However, as with most problems, the mice problem did not go away by itself. One day I was shocked into action. I went down to the storeroom, noticed a hole in a dog food bag and in my usual quick manner grabbed the bag to move it. Two mice scooted between my legs. I jumped as though shot, skedaddled upstairs for my billfold and drove to town for mouse traps. We set traps, with some success, for several nights.

A week or so later the clinic door opened slowly. The old gentleman tottered in, looking despondent, and again with the thin, orange and white cat under his arm and leading the cocker.

"I want this one," he lightly jerked the dog's leash, "put to sleep. I want you to keep the cat, please. My wife is worse and our son insists we move in with him. We can't bring the animals."

"I'm sorry to hear that. Of course we'll put Buster to sleep. He looks like he's had a long, happy life."

I swallowed, not wanting a cat, and particularly not a cat with four declawed paws. A declawed cat meant a house cat.

Our dog, Butterscotch, stayed in one end of the clinic, and we allowed her on a rug by the kitchen door. That was enough.

"I'm not sure about us keeping Bugs."

"But you said you liked this cat," the well-dressed old man said, and looked me in the eye.

I relented, unable to refuse his request straight out. "I'll check with my husband and see what he says. If we can't take him, perhaps we can find someone who will."

"I'll just leave them with you then," he answered. "You'll all enjoy Bugs."

Home from school and doing their chores, the girls noticed Bugs immediately and asked about him. They were ecstatic when hearing the situation and started right in presenting their case.

"But Mom," Jill said. "We *need* a cat. There's mice downstairs."

"Yes," echoed Kay. "Mice. I'm afraid I'll step on one when I jump out of bed. Yuck," she said as she grimaced.

"That cat can't catch mice. He hasn't any claws." But I felt myself wavering.

How many inflections can a child put into the words, "but Mom," I wondered, while I listened to both girls tell me why we should keep Bugs.

"But Mom, we'll keep him downstairs."

"But Mom, we'll take care of him."

"But Mom, even if he can't catch mice he can scare them away."

"I'll talk to Papa, but don't count on it," I said with resignation.

Fred did not help. "It's up to you. I just don't want that cat up here on the furniture. When I sit down I don't want to get up all covered with cat hair."

"Can we keep him?" Jill and Kay begged. "You'll never know he's there. We're the ones who clean our room."

That much was true. I didn't clean downstairs, just ordered it done, with mixed results. Though lax about housekeeping, I did know the girls would take care of Bugs. Their many other well-cared for pets testified to that. The mother in me relented and gave them permission to keep the cat.

For all his agility with his paws, Bugs was an awkward cat. Jumping from the bed to dresser he either fell ignominiously on his back or landed with a great thump. He'd recover quickly and look around, his big eyes asking us not to notice.

A few days after Jill and Kay settled him into the basement, Kay came running upstairs. "Bugs caught a mouse. He ate it," she said excitedly. "Yuck." Bugs also eliminated the basement of crickets, crunching them noisily and making Kay wince.

As Bugs continued to catch and eat mice, we stopped setting traps and let him go at them. Seven was the last count I remember. Jill and Kay claimed they once saw him with one mouse under each paw and one in his mouth! This just *might* be an exaggeration.

When it looked as though Bugs had solved the mouse problem, I took courage in hand, went to the storeroom and cleaned it thoroughly. The girls could jump out of bed without the mouse squishing worry. No more mice ever again.

Maybe because of his diet being supplemented by mice and crickets, the skinny orange and white cat's digestive system rebelled often. He ate what the girls fed him, but likely as not would throw up immediately afterward. Fred dosed him with mineral oil and wormed him in case he had hair balls or worms, but neither helped. Jill, who laid the largest claim on this feline creature, discovered if they fed him a small amount more often he did better, and they patiently continued this regimen.

The old man foretold the future correctly when he said, "You'll all enjoy Bugs."

PEACHES

Once Jill had the opportunity to show off her enthusiasm for horses, a passion Kay did not completely share. Some friends of ours, a couple and their son, stopped on their way from Minnesota to Alaska. The city boy, about the same age as our girls, begged to ride Peaches.

This horse was patient and careful with children. She'd even stop and wait if one started to lose their balance or if something didn't feel just right. We assured his parents of their son's safety. Peaches sedately walked several times around the pasture while the young man rode, proudly smiling at his watching parents.

Then Jill decided to show her horse off, and took over the reins. Now, as I said, Peaches was a good kid's horse, but her previous owner trained her for barrel racing and rode her in rodeos. She could really pour on the juice and go around corners when she felt the rider on her knew her business.

Jill trotted Peaches down to the back fence line, then turned and gave her the reins. The horse galloped madly down the straight-of-way, heading directly toward the visitors, who stood, safely they thought, on the opposite side of the fence. Seeing the horse speeding right toward them, they retreated, expecting horse and rider to crash into the fence. At the last second Jill reined Peaches in. The horse applied her brakes, coming to a sliding stop, her hind quarters lowered and dust flying.

Before the young man had time to articulate his desire to

have another go, his parents bundled him into the car and headed for Alaska.

SEIZURES AND SUBTERFUGE

"It's important you follow a strict feeding regimen with Butterscotch," the family veterinarian instructed his minions. "Her seizures indicate a low blood sugar problem. Give her one of these," he said, as he set a can of Prescription Diet on the counter, "and a couple of cups of this," indicating a sack of dry food. "Feed her twice a day, the canned in the morning the dry in the evening. Understand?"

"Yes, Papa. We will."

The dog's seizures scared all of them, making them anxious to obey instructions.

To a point. Not long after this, as we started to settle down in the living room with popcorn and cocoa, Joel announced, "I want to stay in the kitchen."

"Why?"

"Just because."

Puzzled, we set his popcorn and cocoa down on the kitchen table and went into the other room. Butterscotch was only allowed on her rug by the kitchen door. Unknown to Joel, Fred sat where he saw Joel reflected in the dining area's glass door. It didn't take much sleuthing to solve this little mystery. Joel ate a kernel of popped corn, then cautiously threw a couple at Butterscotch, who stood with her mouth open and her tail wagging enthusiastically.

"Are you feeding Butterscotch, Joel?"

"No, Papa." The boy's activities ceased for a bit, only to

resume.

"Are you feeding the dog, Joel?"

"No, Papa."

Fred set aside his popcorn, rose to his feet and went into the kitchen to straighten out his lying son.

It was harder to catch Kay in the act, being older and more clever than her brother, but circumstantial evidence convicted her. Kay loved cookies and our cookie jar had a unique sound when someone lifted the lid.

Butterscotch liked cookies as much as Kay. Why did Butterscotch, every time the cookie jar clicked its peculiar little click, immediately stand up, wag her tail, and pant with anticipation? Even Bugs, the cat, if he happened to be around, recognized the sound of the cookie jar and came prancing into the kitchen. Kay worked cleverly, all right, but we knew . . . .

FAMILY TIME

All dressed up and no place to go because hubby's
out on a call. Color her *carefully.*
Dr. Robert M. Miller Cartoon

We tried to give our children the time and attention they
needed, but our business didn't keep nine to five hours. Our
family hours kept getting sucked into the veterinary work.
Many times the entire family would be ready to go someplace
for the day and the phone would ring, or someone would drive

up the driveway. Not always would the entire day be ruined, but our tempers got frayed just by waiting.

I suppose we either got interrupted more because the house and clinic were together, or it just seemed like it because we were on the scene. However, since the kids were in and out of the clinic, both Fred and I saw more of them than we would have, had the clinic and home been separate.

Opportunities for Fred to spend one-on-one time with his offspring were especially limited. They felt his influence mostly as teacher/instructor. My assistance with homework was only called for when it involved rote memory—anything scientific or mathematical Fred accepted as his responsibility. Jill and Kay did not always meet his attempts with enthusiasm. "I ask Papa a simple question and get a half hour's lecture," they both complained. When they listened, they learned.

Most of my "alone" time with the kids involved trips to Missoula, both for shopping trips and medical journeys. There were many disadvantages to the fact Jill needed orthopedic devices to correct her pigeon-toed feet, braces to straighten her teeth, and contacts to correct her vision, all at an early age. To a degree, the time we spent together offset these disadvantages. We combined doctor's appointments, shopping trips, and business errands. Rain, snow, sleet or shine, we'd get up early and head down to Missoula, an 85 mile trip over what Grandma Jennie called, "treacherous mountain roads."

While I drove, Jill, as she got older, or Jill and Kay, if the latter skipped school or it was a summer expedition, organized the day.

"Let's see," went a typical conversation. "If we stop and get what Papa needs at the Farmers Co-op on the way in, then go downtown to the Mercantile and look for jackets, we should have time to go to the shoe store and get running shoes." They numbered the list as they talked. "We should eat lunch before we cross the river for our doctor's appointment."

"When we're on the other side of the river we'll stop at K-Mart," Jill said firmly.

K-Mart sold cheap copies of books, which she avidly collected. Even when she didn't come along to Missoula, she entrusted me with her hoarded allowance and instructed me as to exactly which book she wanted. "And being we have winter outfits on the list, let's check out the new dress shop on Main Street."

"I think we'll look for new winter dress outfits for you first," I informed them, "that's always the worst."

SMILES ALL AROUND

Food, shelter and clothing make up the essentials for living. The first two most girls take for granted. Clothing, to them, is by far the most important. Except for my girls.

Because of the long trip to Missoula, shopping days started early and ended late. Anxious to find time to get the always lengthy list completed, I'd head down the sidewalk, bent forward at the waist and nearly running.

"Hey Mom, wait up," Jill would yell. I'd slow momentarily, then speed up.

"I'm gasping for breath," came from Kay.

Turning my head, I'd grin back at them and say, "You girls are the track stars. Why can't you keep up with your old mother?" But I'd try harder to slow down.

Buying jeans and tee shirts and sweatshirts and running shoes was not a problem. Any old jeans, tees, or sweatshirts would do. No brand name fussiness, not much problem with fit. Running shoes were a pleasure. Both girls liked to buy running shoes; even dress shoes were okay with them. However, a skirt and top or dress showed up on the list occasionally. Or a dress coat.

These purchases elicited moans and sulks and, "I don't like it" always said in a whiny voice. If I wasn't careful, they would buy something just to get the list completed, not planning to ever wear the item. Returning purchases was not an option.

On this particular fall day, dress outfits were first on the list.

"Hey, look, Mom, there's the new shop." Jill pointed across the downtown street. "Let's try that."

I saw the purple canopy over the door, the gold lettering on the window, the beautiful mannequin posing in the latest style. It all screamed "Expensive." The girls crossed the street and entered the shop before I voiced my objections.

"May I help you?" a young clerk asked. She, with her cashmere sweater, gold necklace, wool skirt, and high, skinny heels, looked as expensive as the canopy, the lettering, and the mannequin. Soft background music played. Sweaters lay neatly on walnut tables, and jewelry gleamed in glass cases. Even the air, wafting through, smelled the green smell of money. While we weren't on poverty level, I was usually careful about the pennies.

"We need winter outfits. Something dressy," Jill informed her.

That was all it took. The young woman looked them over, asked their sizes, and all three slowly wound through the shop, treading daintily on the soft carpet.

"How do you like this?" the young saleslady asked, holding a skirt up. "Let's see how this color looks on you," she remarked after choosing a sweater to go with the skirt. "Hum, yes. What do you think?"

After finding skirts and sweaters for both, she cocked her head and looked thoughtful. "Let's try these on, okay?" She opened the doors to two fitting rooms, and after the girls went to try on the clothes, I noticed her checking more items on a counter. I opened my mouth to say, "enough," but before I got that simple word out, she was handing things over the top of the fitting room doors.

"Vests," I heard her say. "You should have vests. A vest will tie everything together."

Giving up, I sat in one of the comfortable, contemporary chairs, a soft mauve color, dollar signs dancing in my head, watching as the girls modeled each outfit. They sashayed in front of me, eyes alight, smiling, just a bit self-conscious in the finery. Their enthusiasm caught me also. My girls, my tomboy girls, were actually having fun on a shopping trip!

Ready to go, each daughter with a skirt, a long sleeved cowl-necked sweater and a vest, the girls beamed with the thought of their new, beautiful clothes. The clerk beamed with the thought of a hefty commission. The MasterCard people beamed as they totaled figures in their gray cubicles, and yes, I beamed with pride at my lovely daughters–and the thought of a leisurely lunch before we had to move on to the next item on the list.

DOG LAKE CACOPHONY

Some family time took place at Dog Lake, later renamed the more elegant title of Rainbow Lake. Dog Lake boasted only a few campsites. Its allure for most locals consisted of the fish they could pull from it, both summer and winter. To us, the main attraction was the fact it was only ten miles from home.

Tourists motored by between Spokane, Washington and Glacier National Park, pulling their RV's, unaware of the beautiful little lake hidden by trees. As a result, the few campsites sat unoccupied, and we could make a snap decision to camp and still be sure of a campsite.

"Let's go camping at Dog Lake," suggested Fred one fine spring day. Lambing and calving season just over, a couple of relaxing days at the lake sounded great. All of us made fast work of camping preparations, and soon we pulled into the campground. A small camper/trailer occupied by an older couple squatted in one campsite, the others only had ghosts of visitors past sitting in the form of ashes in the campfire rings.

We took our time as we put up the tent and inflated the mattresses, enjoying the quietness of the area and the smell of the pine trees, an aroma the companies that make things like PineSol try to copy, with miserable success.

Suddenly a raucous noise split the silence. Ackkk, Ackkk. Ackkk. We jumped at the sound of the chain saw, and all eyes turned to stare at the destroyer of quiet. Our camping neighbor had decided to cut some wood.

"I hope he doesn't keep that up," I yelled to Fred.

"Nah," he yelled back, "he'll just cut a little wood for a bonfire."

Wrong. Our innocent-looking elderly neighbor cut wood all afternoon and stacked it against his trailer.

The noise of the chainsaw rang in our ears, and the gas smell fouled the air. We even heard the chainsaw in the distance while we sat by the lake watching the girls fish. When we meandered back and I saw the amount of wood stacked by the trailer, I gasped, "My goodness, he's getting in a winter's supply."

"A peaceful camping trip," remarked Fred bitterly. "I wish a Forest Service ranger would make a surprise visit."

Finally at suppertime the old gent put away his chainsaw and disappeared inside the trailer. Quiet at last. Breathing a sigh of relief, we prepared a bonfire for a marshmallow roast, and dug out the bent-to-shape wire clothes hangers we used for these events. Fred and all three kids competed to see who roasted theirs most perfectly. None of them cared much about eating their golden confections, so I cadged most of theirs and ate mine any old way they happened to come out of the fire–black or golden. Perfection has never been my goal, sad to say.

After the marshmallow roast we settled in our sleeping bags and let the fresh air and quiet noises of nature lull us off to sleep.

"KaBoom," came from the heavens, and five startled bodies in five sleeping bags rose into the air. The wind blew and raindrops plopped noisily on the tent.

"KaBooom," came another crack of thunder, shaking the ground beneath us. Lightning filled the tent with intermittent sharp light. A storm. A doozy of a storm. I wondered whether the tent would stand or whether the ground itself would stay secure; each peal of thunder seemed louder and made the earth shake harder than the one before. There is nothing quite as awesome as a thunder and lightning storm when the only thing between you and the elements is a thin canvas. Canvas makes a flimsy shield.

Fred got out of his sleeping bag, let Butterscotch in from the storm, and made sure our belongings did not touch the sides of the tent where they would absorb moisture. The storm lasted most of the night, and when dawn broke, we all rose, bleary-eyed and sleepy.

Our spirits rose with the sun. A green, fresh world awaited us, with drops of rain still hanging from the needles and leaves of trees. The usual forest sounds; birds chirping, bees buzzing at their day's work, wet leaves dripping, played a symphony to the soul. Wood smoke and bacon aroma lifted high in the clean air and I wondered why it wasn't arousing our neighbors. Not that I wanted it to. I'd have been happy if they stayed quietly in bed all day.

After our normal, huge camping breakfast of pancakes, bacon and eggs, Jill and Kay took their fishing poles and walked out into the lake, while Fred, Joel and I relaxed. It was Saturday morning, and we expected more company in the campground—we just didn't quite expect what came—a black pickup full of young teenagers. It stopped in front of our neighbor's camper and five boys piled out of the cab.

"Do you see what I see?" asked Fred.

Bikes. Motorized dirt bikes filled the back of the pickup. Suddenly this camping trip struck us as the funniest thing ever. We laughed, as the newcomers roared around the campground in high gear, making dust and noise and having a great time.

"So much for a peaceful, quiet camping trip—chainsaws, thunder and dirt bikes. Home is going to be peaceful and quiet after all this," I said.

MOVING REMEMBRANCE

It was only twelve acres of Montana: twelve acres of sagebrush, a hardy kind of yellow wild flower whose name I never remembered, Mt. Baldy in the background–and mosquitoes.

Our minds and our bodies argued for over a year about whether the veterinary work with the cattle and horses was or was not getting too difficult. Our bodies won. A move was imminent. We had worked together, first as husband and wife, then as a family, as we chose a few acres on which to build, then built a house, a clinic, a clientele and friendships.

What would be the dollar value? To whom could we sell?

Who would take care of it? No one else knew the birthing process that started with those few acres of land, those loads of concrete and piles of lumber. Nobody understood the pride we felt in its development. For seventeen years this place had been our life—children and laughter, children and tears, celebrations and tragedies—events that changed us, matured us.

Someone moving in would see a neat, three bedroom rambler, beige with white trim. We saw a house with corners full of Kay's paper doll families and Jill's books. We saw a living room where Sue labored over her plastic chickens, pigs and horses, trying to get them to stand straight in their pens, and a basement where Joel and his friends rammed the walls with various foot and hand powered vehicles. We saw a bright, comfortable and easy to clean house. Just the house we wanted.

Someone moving in would think the clinic "efficient." They might even be able to point out what they thought were mistakes in its design. To us the clinic meant hours of poring through veterinary journals to find plans of other clinics, as we measured and drew and re-measured and re-drew, finding out how many square feet a cattle chute was, how wide an alleyway must be, how much room it would take for a surgery table, and how it should be placed so the cattle and horses would not balk but go obediently in to be strapped down. It wasn't just "efficient" to us. To us it was perfection. How do you sell perfection?

For someone else living on these acres, the windbreak on the windward side of the house and clinic would be "protective." To us, the windbreak meant sweating in the sun as we fought off the mosquitoes and planted 600 individual trees that looked like dead, twelve inch twigs. To us the windbreak was buffalo berry, sand cherry, honeysuckle bushes, green ash, American elm, Scotch pine, and Russian olive trees, graduating from bushes to large growing trees and coming back down again in the same way. To us, the windbreak meant handmade dams of dirt around each tree and each tree watered with a bucket and hose. To us, the windbreak wasn't just "protective." It was a miracle.

A welcoming house, a workable clinic, wind defying trees, all set in Montana's sagebrush-spiced air, with 7,493 feet of Mt. Baldy overseeing our activities. Let's remember the mosquitoes.

FARGO, NORTH DAKOTA

Large animal veterinary medicine is not for wimps. We started our days early, checking the sick animals in the clinic before Fred left on his ranch calls. He gulped meals down any time he could take a few minutes, and augmented them by racing into the house to raid the cookie jar.

Mike Marrinan, a local man recently graduated from vet school, expressed an interest in buying our practice. This started Fred thinking about a career change, and a few days later I showed him the Sanders County Ledger.

"Look, Fred, a veterinarian is moving to Plains. That's going to hurt our small animal practice. He'll get not only our Plains but also our Thompson Falls clients. At least the majority of them won't drive past him to come here."

Fred read the article. "Ouch. And Mike is eating into our cattle practice in Camas Prairie by treating his family and friends' livestock. Maybe we should seriously consider selling him our practice."

When we talked it over with the kids, the questions came fast and furious.

"Why should we move?"

"Where will we go?"

"What will you do, Papa?"

"What will happen to Santa Claus? We won't be able to move a milk cow."

"The sheep can go to market." This statement proved the

girls had no particular attachment to their flock of sheep.

"But what about the horses? And Butterscotch and Bugs?"

We answered their questions as best we could, and even though they did not like the idea of moving, they didn't have much choice, as our adult votes carried more weight than theirs. In early spring of 1977 Mike and Peggy Marrinan bought our house and clinic.

The horses were sold, the sheep went to the auction market in Missoula. Doug Jackson bought the beloved Jersey cow.

"Butterscotch and Bugs will move with us," I assured the girls and Joel.

***

Bugs, fully grown, still skinny and still with the large, inquisitive eyes, moved with us to a rented house in town. Even after his gangly adolescent period, he stayed clumsy, and the girls laughed at his antics and his resulting injured dignity. They continued to feed him small portions often, and in the strange house, had to put his litter pan deep into the closet before he would use it. He needed privacy, Jill explained when I worried about the owner's reaction. No doubt about it, Bugs the cat needed a psychologist.

We rented the Hot Springs house for two months while the kids finished the school year. Fred spent those two months job hunting, starting with writing resumes. These I laboriously typed up, computers having not been invented yet, or at least not being used by the common people.

The community held a good-bye party for us in the multi-purpose room of the school. Roy Merritt was the emcee, which increased the emotions of the evening. Roy and Jean's young daughter had been killed in a car accident after our Sue's death. Nothing was said about the accidents, but all knew and remembered. Many ranchers spoke good things about Fred, and after the evening, Mike Marrinan said, "I have big shoes to fill."

Jill and Kay's classmates came through with parties for them, and Jolene Jacobson's daughter, Bevra, raided her comic book drawer and brought a grocery sack full of comics for Joel. "To read on your long trip," she told him.

Before I married Fred and moved with him to Hot Springs, the longest I had lived in one location was four years. Moving from this area and the people in it meant leaving a place I truly called home. My roots reached deep into the clay soil on top of which we built our house. One of our children was buried just down the road. Yet my gut feeling insisted the move, the change, would be beneficial for all of us. We left. Our Minnesota relatives would take turns putting up with us while Fred continued being interviewed for possible jobs.

Butterscotch and Bugs turned into reasonable travel partners, and no one turned us out because of them. Even with the relatives opening their doors, the summer turned into an expensive ordeal. One interview after another first lifted and then dashed our hopes. Fall came. We decided to enroll the kids in school at Mapleton, Minnesota, where my folks lived.

Shortly after we enrolled the kids in school, Fred received two job possibilities. One meant a move to Silver Spring, Maryland, to work for the Food and Drug Administration, the other to Fargo, North Dakota, to work as a field veterinary medical officer for APHIS (Animal, Plant Health Inspection Service).

We didn't deliberate long. Moving our three country-raised kids to a huge metropolitan area seemed like too big a step. North Dakota sounded friendlier. This turned out to be a good choice. Jill, Kay, and Joel all settled in at school, I found a part time job, Butterscotch adjusted to being walked rather than being let loose, and Bugs made the downstairs his domain.

Joel and I poked around in a pet store one day. "Hey, Mom, look at that," he exclaimed, pointing to a gerbil habitat display. "I want some gerbils and some tubes and things for them. Please, Mom. I'll pay from my allowance."

His allowance stretched to cover part of the cost of two gerbils, one new aquarium (which joined his old one) and a connecting tube.

"My gerbils need a wheel and an exercise ball," he soon announced. By saving his allowance and birthday money, his bankroll again, "burned a hole in his pocket," as my dad would say. Resignedly, I brought him back to the pet store.

"Hey, look, I can get another tube and this neat little room here at the corner."

After these additions, which made the habitat look similar to the skywalk linking buildings in downtown Minneapolis, those of us who routinely cleaned the whole affair, Kay, Jill or myself, cried, "enough" and halted construction.

Bugs lived downstairs with Jill and Kay. All family members did not at all times ensure they latched the downstairs door securely. Occasionally a skinny, orange and white leg pushed it open and two large eyes emerged to investigate this larger world. The gerbils interested him. Maybe they brought memories of his heyday in Montana when he won the title Hero of the Day by catching mice. We'd surprise him in Joel's room, intently watching the caged rodents cross in the tube from one aquarium to the other.

No one ever doubted the intelligence of Bugs the cat. Whenever he'd accomplish a sneak foray upstairs and into Joel's domain, he knew enough to wait until the most opportune moment, then one quick swipe with his paw, and down came the tube. Someone always arrived in time to avert catastrophe.

Then came the day when no rescuer arrived. Bugs broke the tube and caught an unlucky gerbil. How long the cat played with and tortured it is in question. When we arrived home, we saw the open basement door and Bugs making a run for it, gerbil in mouth.

"Hey, Bugs caught a gerbil," Kay yelled.

Both girls scrambled to snatch the cat, who thought this an exciting diversion from his normally dull life. Jill and Kay caught Bugs and extricated the small gerbil. He was still alive, but barely. Fred offered to put it out of its misery, but the girls and Joel objected.

"Well, then I guess you'll have to feed it sugar water from a dropper every hour or so and see what happens," Fred said.

"We've gotta put that cat to sleep," Joel said, with a catch in his voice.

"He was only doing what nature intended him to do," replied Jill. "We can't euthanize him for that."

"Your gerbil will live," Kay assured her brother. "Wait and see."

The girls set their alarm clocks at night and got up several times to tend to their patient. In a few days they deposited Mr. Gerbil back with his brother, good as new. Everyone learned their lesson. We all carefully shut the basement door.

***

Our income went downhill after selling the practice. A starting salary for a government employee is small and we learned what it is to pinch pennies. Unfortunately Bugs did not cooperate.

Jill came to me, a worried look on her face. "Mom, Bugs is using his pan every few minutes."

Being a veterinarian's daughter she knew that meant trouble. Fred was in Pembina working at the Canadian port of entry, and it was my decision.

"Mom, he must get to a veterinarian right away," pleaded Jill.

I knew that. I also knew that, even if a vet cleared his urinary tract this time, the problem would resurface. Special food might help, but probably not head off another bout of urethral calculi.

Faced with a choice of two rebellious teenagers, or a confrontation with the father of the family over expenses, I chose the latter. Even though Jill promised to help with the expense, I knew Fred's deep and abiding belief; a pet should be a pet only as long as it was not a financial burden on the family. We all weathered the storm. Even Bugs survived.

***

A dog's lifetime is short. By the time Joel was wheelchair-bound, Butterscotch was middle-aged. When we moved from Montana to North Dakota, from the country to the city, Butterscotch accepted her house confinement with the same submissiveness Joel exhibited in the imprisonment of his spirited mind in his unresponsive body. Giving his dog the attention she craved tested Joel's ingenuity.

One quiet day, as I sat and read in the living room, Joel sat by the kitchen door, scratching under Butterscotch's ears.

"Kay," I heard him ask, "will you put one of my gerbils in the exercise ball?"

"Okay. Where do you want the ball?"

"Here in the kitchen. It rolls better."

Kay put a gerbil in the ball and set it on the kitchen floor. The gerbil ran busily, rolling the plastic ball around the floor.

Out of the corner of my eye I saw Butterscotch stretch out on her rug, head on her front paws, eyes following the ball's movement. We did not allow her off that rug.

"Butterscotch, wouldn't you like to play with that gerbil?" asked Joel. He maneuvered his wheelchair so the gerbil would go closer to the dog.

"Look at that gerbil, Butter. Such a tasty morsel. One gulp.

Come and see."

The dog wagged her tail, watching the gerbil attentively. She stayed on the rug.

"C'mon, Butter. Mom won't care. She doesn't like the gerbils. Says they stink."

He turned his wheelchair adroitly and guided the exercise ball closer to the dog's nose. Butterscotch's whiskers twitched. Jill came into the kitchen for a snack.

"Joel, why do you harass Butterscotch?"

"I'm not harassing her. We're playing. She likes it."

"She's frustrated. She knows she's not supposed to catch that gerbil. Poor dog." Jill reached down and patted the dog, then left, munching her apple.

"That Jill doesn't know anything, does she Butterscotch? That Jill thinks you can't catch this gerbil. Of course you can catch this gerbil. Easier'n those gophers you used to chase in Montana."

The gerbil had moved away during the interruption. Joel now steered it close to the dog again; too close. Under duress, Butterscotch forgot her training, jumped up and hit the ball with her nose. It fell apart and the gerbil ran.

"Jill! Kay! The gerbil is loose! Catch the gerbil!"

Butterscotch retreated to her rug, dismayed at the commotion. Joel's long- suffering sisters searched for the gerbil, grumbling. I kept my nose in my book.

***

In spite of the girls' fussing and arguing with Joel, they never seemed embarrassed to be seen with him, and pushed his wheelchair most every place they went.

Sports rated high. "Hey, Papa, there's a hockey game tonight. We're playing Crookston. Let's all go."

"It's awfully cold to take Joel out."

168

"He's tough. He can take it. Can't you?" Kay ruffled Joel's hair, as she talked, something he hated but couldn't do anything about. "Besides you bought him that insulated snow suit. He'll be fine." We went to the game.

Jill, looking through the paper one day said, "Hey Mom. This sounds like a good play. 'Anything Goes.' It says, 'Cole Porter's delicious music stars in this whimsical Broadway musical.' Let's go."

"I've seen that theater, Jill. It's in an old building with a long flight of steps. Papa is busy. We can't get Joel up those steps."

"Yes, we can. Kay and I will haul the wheelchair up, and you can carry Joel."

They convinced me, and after that first time, we spent many entertaining evenings at the old community theater.

***

During the time we live in Fargo, Joel and Fred went on a "stag" camping trip with Reed Boelter and his dad. They came back with stories of a grand time, so us females decided to take our turn. We'd leave the males behind and go on a, "powder puff" camping trip.

"You won't even get the tent up," scoffed Joel, mischief in his eyes.

Stung, the girls replied, "Who says?"

"I say."

We chose Itasca State Park in Minnesota, packed the van and set out. At the park we drove around, deciding where to pitch the tent, hoping to get close to Lake Itasca. Jill started to moan at sight of the lake. "Why didn't we bring our fishing poles? Surely they have boats to rent."

"We can rent a boat and go out even without poles," I said.

"But we can't fish. I want to fish."

She forgot her pique as we set up camp, and she took the

lead in figuring out which tent poles went where and what came next, her voice muffled as she fought under the canvas. As we struggled with the tent, we discussed whether this was the spot where we camped on our first trip to Itasca. Our memories were not that precise, but we did remember the 'coon incident, and we stopped our work and started reminiscing.

"Remember, Mom, how Butterscotch started barking at that 'coon in the middle of the night?" asked Kay. "Woke all of us up."

"Sure do. She barks so seldom, Papa immediately unzipped his sleeping bag and grumbled up to investigate."

"That guy had a brand new Bronco. Pop shined his flashlight on it, then made a quick u-turn and came back," remembered Jill, 'Hey, come and look at this,' he told us."

A raccoon had chewed a hole in the Plexiglass-type top of the Bronco parked at the neighboring campsite, then dropped through the hole to feast on stashed food supplies. About that time Butterscotch woke and set up a clamor, scaring the thief, who knew the only way out was the way he'd come in.

"Yes," I added to the story, "The 'coon got his front feet and his head up through the hole, but his fat belly simply stuck, like Pooh Bear, half in and half out. Unlike Pooh Bear, he had no Christopher Robin or Rabbit to happily read him stories until he got skinny."

"I remember," Kay said, "that when Papa woke the peacefully sleeping neighbor, that guy danced around his vehicle, shouting at the raccoon, opening the doors and trying to shoo the animal out."

All the commotion terrified the already fear-struck raccoon. We watched him as he hunched his back and clawed with his front legs, trying to spring up and out. In desperation he voided his bladder and emptied his bowels, sending urine and fecal material all over the inside of the distraught camper's Bronco. That did the trick. His belly collapsed just enough he freed himself and exited the crime scene. The man surveyed the damage, gloom on his face, and I suspect that when we slept quietly, he stayed awake, rehearsing the story he'd tell his insurance agent.

But, memories aside, if we were to sleep on this trip, we needed to finish the tent job. With much teasing and laughter, we managed to get it up. So what if it looked a tad lopsided. In case Joel questioned our veracity, we took a picture of it.

Itasca Park is where the Mississippi River starts as a tiny stream. We jumped the Mississippi as a matter of form, as we'd done it before, looked over the exhibits in the visitor's center, and enjoyed a walk in the woods.

Calm, blue Lake Itasca continued to tease the girls, making us drive to the boat rental office. They rented both canoes and rowboats. Paddling a canoe with a dog and three know-nothing canoeists, seemed too much like putting our lives in jeopardy. In comparison, a rowboat looked much more seaworthy. A rowboat it was.

The rental office sat high on a bank, overlooking the dock area. Needing to watch activities on the dock, the proprietors had put in large windows along that side. A long narrow inlet led to the lake and the dock jutted out the side of this inlet.

Butterscotch led the way, and we clambered down the bank to the fishy smelling inlet, our life preservers slung over our shoulders. I surveyed the rowboat dubiously. "That thing looks big and clumsy. You think we can make it go?"

"No problem. We just row," Kay assured me.

We put on our life preservers, adjusting the straps carefully. Jill and Kay possibly could swim to safety if we upset. My demise would be certain.

Down at the dock, the high bank hid the lake, but blue sky, bright sun, and good spirits made us laugh lightheartedly as we prepared to board the boat. Some instinct told Butterscotch that swimming was not on the agenda, and she jumped into the sturdy craft even before we did. She bounced around, tipping the vessel this way and that, until her brain processed our instructions to stop and be still. She stopped, poised in the front, her nose and tail both up in the air, ready for adventure.

Kay and Jill settled themselves by the oars and struggled to put them into the oarlocks. I untied the boat, and we were off! Well, not quite. "How do we back this thing out of here?" asked Jill.

"Just put your rower in," her sister answered promptly.

"That won't work, we'll both have to go at the same time."

They pushed away from the dock amid bickering and laughter, and managed to get the front of the boat headed in the right direction. It, however, refused to go straight. First it veered off in one direction; then with shouted instructions from each other, they got it to obey momentarily before it started veering off in the other direction.

Wiping my eyes on my shirttail, I managed to say between bouts of laughter, "Can you imagine what those men in the office think of us?"

This started the girls off again, and the more laughter, the more erratic our progress. Butterscotch, excited by our hilarity, decided to jump around again, creating even more confusion.

After rowing far more distance than required, we staggered out of the inlet and into the lake. Though it had appeared calm, we discovered even the small waves impeded our progress. Jill and Kay were getting the hang of rowing, so we rowed for a while, taking care not to get too far from shore, then headed back into the inlet, docking with relief, mingled with satisfaction. I imagined the men in the office giving a sigh, glad they wouldn't have to go to our rescue.

TEXAS, HERE WE COME

"A high school graduate could do this," Fred complained occasionally. The contrast between a busy veterinary practice and a government regulatory job was immense. Fred had stuck it out for over two years when a notice from the government came in the mail. They wanted a veterinarian interested in economics and would put him through graduate school, on salary, all expenses paid. Fred sent in his application and the government accepted him into the program. A move to Texas was imminent.

"I do not want to move," declared Jill, engrossed in her senior year of high school. "I'll stay with Wixo's."

"Jill, you're part of our family. We want you with us," I said.

I understood Jill's feelings, but knew Fred would never get another opportunity like this. Kay felt the same as Jill but was not as vocal. Joel was game for any move. It was near the middle of their school term, so Fred went to Texas by himself and rented a room from a group of women.

"A bunch of women?" I asked. "According to the apostle Paul you're supposed to 'abstain from any appearance of evil,' and here you are with a harem."

He laughed. "Wait until you see them. And they're a bunch of pigs. I spent a couple hours scrubbing the bathroom before I felt comfortable enough to pee in the pot."

During the time Fred set himself up and started his classes at Texas A&M, the kids finished their semester and I finished the

Fargo house sale.

In between classes and studying, Fred looked at houses, hoping to find one I would approve of when I flew down. During Christmas vacation I left Joel in the care of his sisters and went to Texas. Fred had found three possibilities, and I picked an older, four bedroom, two bath brick house.

"That's the one house I didn't think you'd pick," my husband told me. "It's dark."

"It seems like it would suit our family the best," I told him. "After we trim the bushes in front of the windows and I do some painting, it will brighten up. There's more living room space, and a dining room. The halls are large enough for Joel's wheelchair. Space in the bathroom that Joel would use is a problem, but we can work around that."

Housing settled, I returned to Fargo and started the moving process, vowing this time I'd get it right. First I sorted through the closets and cupboards, which wasn't too difficult as I did that often. Then, I gathered anything from each area of the house that I would want to unpack at the same time, and put those in piles so we'd pack them all together.

In spite of their bad feelings about the move, Jill and Kay pitched in to help get things ready for the movers and gave me the moral support I needed. Our efforts paid off. It was a smooth move.

After the movers left, we packed the brown and tan Dodge van carefully, making room for the cat cage, the dog, and the gerbils (confined to one aquarium for the trip), and some houseplants I foolishly tried to move. This government paid, three-day trip, we decided, would not be a rush trip. We would take our time. Between the pets and Joel, rushing wasn't an option anyway.

Every evening the houseplants would have to be taken into the motel room so they wouldn't freeze, then put back into the van the next morning. Butterscotch would have to be walked at least three times during the day, and both her and Bugs, even the gerbils, would need feeding. Every meal for us would be slow also, as we'd have to unload Joel's wheelchair, load him into it, and then wait an excruciatingly long time for him to eat a meal. No, it would not be a quick trip.

Toward the end of our first traveling day, someone called out from the back seat, "Look there's a Holiday Inn with a Holidome. Let's stay there tonight."

Never before had a Holiday Inn made our list of motels, but this time all our expenses would be returned into our checking account, courtesy of the United States government.

"Sounds good to me," I answered as I turned in. We all went swimming or hot tubbing in the Holidome before sinking gratefully in our beds, smelling like chlorine, but feeling like rich vacationers.

Jill and Kay both spelled me off on the driving, even though neither were experienced to any great degree. One of them sat behind the wheel the next day when I noticed the sky ahead of us turning black.

"Looks like snow coming, and it's warm enough it'll be slippery. Do you want me to take over?" I asked.

"I'm okay."

She managed fine. Even my fingernails survived.

Saturday evening came. Forearmed with telephone numbers, we called about Sunday morning meeting. The nice person on the other end of the line gave me good directions, and we all trooped into their house the next morning.

"You'll be in Oklahoma City in time for gospel meeting this afternoon," someone told me after our fellowship meeting. "I can tell you how to get there." I wasn't so sure of trying to find gospel meeting in the big city of Oklahoma City, but I took the directions.

"We'll help find it," the girls volunteered. "It can't be that hard."

Between the map and the written directions, we made it to gospel meeting, safe and on time.

An exasperated Fred met us when we pulled up in front of the apartment he had rented for us to stay in until the movers came to Bryan with our furniture. When we found out why he was upset, all our satisfying, proud feelings about making a safe trip dissipated. He had the key to the apartment, that was true. However, the property manager failed to turn on the electricity and water. The kids were supposed to start school the next day.

"I won't go to school without washing my hair," declared Jill. Kay, looking as stubborn as Jill sounded, agreed. And how was I supposed to cook without any electricity? Things smoothed out when the utilities were turned on the next day, and the day after, all the students were in school. Within a few days the moving van came to the house and we settled into a new routine and environment.

Bugs and Butterscotch adjusted well to their surroundings and the gerbils never seemed to know they transitioned from northerners to southerners. With no basement, we installed Bugs in Jill and Kay's bedroom. He meandered contentedly from window sill to top bunk to bottom bunk, losing his balance more often than not but usually ending right side up.

***

Both Jill and Kay were good drivers. However, their different personalities came into play here. Kay sat up straight and paid attention to the road. Jill sat behind the wheel, relaxed and over confident. It drove me nuts.

Finally she'd had enough of my gentle reminders to pay attention. "I'll have you know," she announced to all in the van. "I am the only driver in this family who has not had an accident."

A few nights later she asked to use the van to go to a party.

Being parents, sleep eluded us, and we heard the van return. After a long pause, Jill stopped by our bedroom door. "Papa," said a penitent voice, "I wrecked the van."

The tone of that forlorn, "Papa" hit our funny bones, and we giggled instead of bawling her out. Fred did make Jill do all the paperwork involved in estimates and police reports, and we teased her unmercifully. Maybe she'd rather have been scolded.

Kay probably never got teased for her driving, but we did tease her about her spoiling of Butterscotch. Butterscotch loved water, except when it came down from the sky. In Texas, when it rained, it poured, to put it mildly. Had the little Morton salt box girl, holding an umbrella, been in Texas during a rain storm, the only thing left of her would be a scrap of yellow dress hung up on the storm sewer.

Through the years Kay had gained the dog's loyalty by giving her consistent care and attention. Butterscotch objected strenuously to going out in the rain, so Kay humored her by "holding her paw" so she'd do her jobs.

"You'll have to go out with her, Kay. She'll never go out if you don't."

"But Mom, it's coming down hard. I don't want to get all wet."

"She doesn't either, but she needs to go out." I smiled at Kay. "It's your fault. You've spoiled her."

So, Kay, grimacing, took a look at the Texas downpour and went to find a jacket to put over her head. She knew the dog had to go out after the long night, and Butterscotch certainly knew the urgency. Wanting company in her misery, Kay was the only person she could count on for support.

Back with her jacket, Kay drew back the yellow drapes covering the sliding door and opened it. The dog looked up at her, then sidled out to the backyard. "Hurry up, Butterscotch," I heard her say resignedly.

It amuses me that, even now, in her forties, Kay always goes out and "holds the paw" of her golden retriever while he does his duties. She still gets teased about it.

JOEL

Apparently the Texas section of the Muscular Dystrophy Association had more money than either the Montana or North Dakota groups, or maybe they were just more generous. At any rate, they offered to outfit Joel with an electric wheelchair.

I'm not sure of the sequence of events, but we ended up at the Scott and White Medical Center in Temple, Texas, where they were to adjust a wheelchair to fit Joel. Don't ask me why he had to stay in the hospital for this to happen, but he did. We left our son, ecstatic about getting new wheels, and went home.

Then came a phone call. A nurse moved Joel, and, in the process, broke his leg. People looking on would think that Fred and I both slung Joel around haphazardly, but that was not the case. Practice makes perfect and we'd had lots of practice. We knew exactly how to move him. I didn't so much blame the nurse, but wondered why, when Scott and White was designated a special Muscular Dystrophy Clinic, they didn't train their employees in the proper way to move patients like Joel.

Fred and I drove up to Temple to see what was up. Joel lay in bed, a huge plaster of paris cast on his leg. When Fred found out where the bone was broken, high on the thigh, and the cast covered his leg from his ankle to about where the break was, and no further, he was furious. It is common knowledge to most people, and especially those in the health care profession, a broken bone must be immobilized below and *above* the break. This orthopedic specialist stopped the heavy cast right at the break.

"Why," Fred asked me, his anger amplifying his words, "Did they put a huge cast on a boy who is unable to move his leg by himself? An Ace bandage would have immobilized the broken bone better."

Of course, he knew asking me such a question was asking the wrong person. No doctor was available to talk to, however, so he said, "I'll call when I get home."

Joel looked at his father. "It's okay. It doesn't hurt. I'll be fine."

What his eyes were saying was, "I want the wheelchair. If there's a big fuss maybe they won't give it to me."

We visited our son for a while, made sure he was comfortable, and left for home. Fred did call, talked to the medical doctor responsible for Joel, who promised to have a lighter, fiberglass cast put on the leg.

Three days later Jill and I drove up to see the patient. I was dismayed, we were both dismayed, by what we saw.

"Haven't they given you a bath of any kind, Joel?" I asked. He shook his head.

"They haven't even brushed his teeth," Jill declared, "and his hair is filthy."

The bed sheets looked like they hadn't been changed either.

"Have they had you up in a chair?"

Again he shook his head. Obviously the nurses were so freaked out about breaking the leg, they simply let him lay in bed. Now I was the one furious. I inspected the new cast.

"Look, Jill, they still took the cast only a inch or two above where they said the break was. That doesn't make sense. I suppose they think that because he can't walk it won't matter."

I turned to Joel. "Why don't we take you home? After your leg heals we can come back and they'll give you your electric wheelchair."

Again, his eyes pleaded with me. "Maybe they won't let me

come back, Mom," he said.

So Jill and I set to work, taking him into the bathroom and washing his hair, brushing his teeth, giving him a sponge bath. I called the nurse's aide in to change the sheets while we worked on Joel.

Personally, I thought when they hospitalized Joel simply to measure for a wheelchair, Scott and White was thinking of the insurance they would collect from our insurance company. They did even better than that. I perused the statements from Blue Cross/Blue Shield and found Scott and White charged them, not only for the ridiculous plaster of paris cast, plus the lighter fiberglass cast, but also the extra days of hospitalization. All because their nurse had not been trained properly.

Joel's broken leg ended up shorter than the other. No other outcome was possible considering the cast the orthopedist put on it. However, it didn't really make any difference.

I abided by Joel's wishes and didn't raise a fuss. He loved his new wheels, and I'm sure he thought the trauma we'd all gone through was well worth it. And we were all happy that he was happy.

There is a postscript to this story. The battery the wheelchair came with was not large enough to last an entire school day. We found a machinist who made a larger battery platform on the back of the chair and he put a second battery on it, so Joel could buzz along for twice as long. When I went to pay for the extra battery and his work, he waved me aside, "No charge. Glad to do it for him."

***

By the time we moved to Texas, I was older and Joel's muscle weakness had worsened. Concerned about my ability to stay in shape so I could continue caring for him, I started to jog.

"You want to go with me to the university jogging trail?" I

asked Joel.

He turned to the dog, "You want to go running, Butter? You do? Okay, let's go."

Since receiving his electric wheelchair, Joel loved going to the university campus, where all the walks and buildings were handicapped accessible. Unloaded from the van, he hummed quietly down the sidewalk.

"O.K. Butter. Come with me." I put the leash on her collar.

The elderly Butterscotch frolicked excitedly around my legs.

"Let's go, old lady."

I set off on a slow jog, Butterscotch at my side. She kept up the first lap around the trail, on the second she pulled ahead of me and, almost imperceptibly, slowed down, forcing me to take shorter steps.

As I neared the sidewalk I saw Joel. What did he think as he sat and watched the students? Tears came to my eyes as I thought of what life could have held for this young man with the wonderful intellect and rare sense of humor.

Joel saw me wave at him and came over.

"Take care of Butter until I finish running." I looped the dog's leash over the arm of the wheelchair.

Butterscotch, panting, laid her head on Joel's knee, and he reached to rub her head.

"What's wrong, ol' girl? Can't keep up anymore, huh? This Texas sun too hot? Can't do whatcha' used to do? Well, neither can I, Butterscotch."

The young man and old dog consoled one another while I finished my run.

***

Jerry Lewis' Muscular Dystrophy summer camps were the highlight of Joel's summers. He went to camps in Montana, North Dakota and now would add Texas to the list. In the process of packing Joel's suitcase for this annual sojourn, I walked toward the bedroom with an armload of his clothes. As I came down the hall, I could hear him and his dad arguing.

"No, Joel, you're not taking Chimp to camp with you." Fred's voice was firm. "You're nearly fourteen. That's too old to play with a stuffed monkey. We should have thrown both Chimp and Penguin out years ago."

"But I don't actually play with Chimp. I just like to have him. Anyway, kids bring all sorts of things to camp."

"Nope. Chimp stays home."

Joel looked at me, obviously wanting me to intervene, but I kept silent, determined to stay out of this argument. Fred was right. Yet I knew Joel filled in some lonely times imagining Chimp and Penguin alive and adventurous.

Joel seemed to accept his dad's orders and started looking through his new clothes. "You got them all marked?" he asked.

"Yep."

Every year after Joel left, the house seemed empty and quiet, particularly to me. I was the only one home during the day, and for years my everyday life had been entwined with his. Camp only lasted a week, however, and soon it was time to meet the bus, unload the slightly grimy camper and his stuff, and haul everything home.

He was tanned and happy. "I got the 'Poorest Puns' award," he announced with pride. "And I had a super-duper counselor this year. He took me swimming every day. And you know, Pop, you told me to drink lots of water 'cause it's hot. One camper didn't, and he had a seizure. I saw it. It was awful. He thrashed around, all you could see of his eyes was the white part." Joel rolled his eyes, trying to demonstrate.

"He looked like he was dying, and the counselors practically had to sit on him to hold him down. Then the ambulance came, and the men hauled him off to the hospital. After that my counselor said he'd never seen anyone drink as much water as I did."

As he talked I opened his suitcase, which smelled like a mixture of sweat and chlorine. On the top of his mostly dirty clothes lay a large, brown envelope. "This must be your annual picture," I said as I took it out.

"Yep," said Joel, with an impish smile. "Our picture and my poorest puns award."

I took out the picture and laid it on the bed. There sat Joel in his wheelchair, front row, his face alight with a "gotcha" grin. Penguin sat on his lap.

"That's Penguin! How did he get in your suitcase?" I asked, puzzled.

Joel shrugged. "You can never tell, Mom, what Chimp's able to do. He couldn't come, but he must've tossed Penguin in when we weren't looking."

***

Physical therapy for Joel may not have been completely useless, but it seemed that way. His muscles continued to lose strength. His core muscles deteriorated enough he could not sit in a chair without leaning over. Eating became a problem as he couldn't lift his arms. Back to Scott and White we went. They didn't hospitalize him this time, we just made two or three trips to Temple to have Joel measured for a fiberglass shell they installed in the electric wheelchair to hold him up.

Then, and this was a first for them, they manufactured braces for his arms, levered so he could lift an eating utensil up to his mouth. Joel felt self-conscious about these braces, but as with them he could feed himself for the most part, he was glad for them. Every bit of self-sufficiency he could have was important. When he wasn't eating, we simply folded the braces back on themselves and strapped them down with Velcro. Writing was difficult for him also, and it was hoped the braces could help with that, but they didn't. Joel continued to write on his own, it just took effort and time.

***

Kay, like always, played with him when his hours needed to be filled. At this age it meant playing board games. Muscular dystrophy might have wrecked his physical prowess, but it didn't affect his mental aptitude. Also, the word losing was not in his vocabulary. Kay liked an occasional victory, but losing didn't bother her. What irritated her, however, was that Joel loved to play checkers, and he always won. Always. Except once.

"I beat you," she announced gleefully, when she jumped Joel's last king. She swept all the checkers into their box.

"You couldn't have," said an incredulous Joel.

"I did. Didn't you see?" Kay did not jump madly around the room. That was not her style. "I beat Joel at checkers," she told everyone around the table that night.

"You did?" said the family in unison.

"Next time you won't win," came from an indignant Joel.

His patient sister had a right to be elated about that particular victory. Grandpa Brateng taught Joel how to play checkers, starting when Joel was very young. At first Grandpa removed one row of his checkers, giving himself a severe handicap. As Joel got better, Grandpa added more checkers to his side of the board. Finally, when his grandson was proficient enough, Grandpa played with a full board, and Joel still won on occasion. Today a box in our storage shed holds a checker's tournament trophy inscribed with Joel's name.

Joel excelled at board games. I've seen him concentrate so hard on a chess game, that sweat broke out on his forehead. Kay continued to play countless games with him, but that was the last time Kay and Joel met over the checker board. Ever after when Joel asked her to play checkers, the answer was, "Nope. I can beat you at checkers."

Off she would go to get the game of her choice, ignoring Joel's exasperated cries of, "Only once. You only beat me once. Let's play again." Any other game Kay played with him, win or lose. That checkers victory was just too sweet.

***

High school in Bryan went well for Joel. The kids were anxious to hold doors open, and helped get his homework and books out from his backpack and onto his writing surface, which hooked to the arms of the wheelchair. His teachers would have excused him from some projects, such as making posters, but we encouraged him to plan them and let Jill work them up.

A friend of Joel's, Dwight Baker, had spina bifida and walked with two unwieldy canes. He was a short, stocky kid, not good looking, but had an outgoing personality and, like Joel, did not feel sorry for himself. Self pity is not an attractive trait, so the lack of a "poor me" attitude made it easier for the nonhandicapped to relate to the two boys.

Sometimes you see a handicapped child, like Dwight, who simply refuses to admit some things are not within his capabilities. Spina bifida did not stop him from walking in a charity walk for spina bifida. With one slow, dragging step after another, he finished the walk.

Dwight and Joel visited with each other during gym class, and Joel came home brimming with ideas for career choices after high school. When Joel related these to me, it put me in a quandary. How far should I go in encouraging him to dream? I didn't want to squelch the hope that, yes, he could look forward to graduation, a career choice, and college; yet reality made me more non-committal than I would have liked. All the research the medical establishment was doing to find a cure for muscular dystrophy only held out a dim "maybe" prospect for future generations.

Joel and Dwight, sitting out gym classes, received unauthorized, extra-curricular sex education. Pregnant, teen-age girls, also sidelined from participating in gym, joined the two boys. Apparently the girls bragged about their sexual exploits. Joel never gave us detailed accounts of the conversations, but every once in a while he'd blurt out some interesting thing, fact or fiction, that emanated from these worldly-wise girls. We'd raise our eyebrows, but figured the less said the better.

**

My folks drove from Minnesota to visit us, and we took them to see the A&M campus, where Fred was studying for his master's degree in economics. The campus, one of Joel's favorite places, was truly accessible to the handicapped. He often went with me to the jogging trail and wheeled along watching squirrels, the college students, and other people out for a bit of exercise. Or he'd go to the student union.

This particular day Grandpa, Kay, and Fred wanted to admire the library, built, like most of the Texas A&M buildings, on a scale worthy of Texas. Fred told Joel he could wander around outside, but stay within calling distance. Mom and I went over to the track where she walked, and I ran my usual three miles. About the time I finished, Kay came running up.

"Have you seen Joel?" she asked.

"No, he was with you guys."

"I thought he'd snuck away to the Union to watch students play video games, but I checked and he isn't there."

So, Mom in her walking shoes and me in my shorts and sweaty tee, with hair straggling all over, went back to the Union to see if we could find the errant boy. Like Kay, I thought the Union the most likely place to find him, as he loved to watch the kids playing ping pong and video games. Kay had missed seeing him, but there he sat, avidly watching a boy playing "Donkey Kong." I immediately lit into him about not obeying his father.

"Why didn't you stay where you were supposed to? If you don't obey we can't trust you."

While I did the upset mother routine, my mother desperately made faces at me behind Joel's back, trying to get me to shut up. I wasn't loud, but she simply didn't want me to scold her poor, handicapped grandson, which made me madder than ever.

"But, Mom," said Joel, when possible to get a word in edgewise, "they said they'd be gone for a while, and I figured it wouldn't matter if I came here for a few minutes. I got stuck in the elevator."

"What?" I asked, calming down a little.

"I got on the elevator with a bunch of students, but they all left on the first floor, and when the elevator stopped at my floor I didn't get out fast enough. The door shut, and I couldn't reach the open button. It took a long time before someone came to use the elevator, and I could get out. I didn't mean to be gone so long."

Kay told him, "I came to find you, Joel, but I must have been on the stairway at the same time you were stuck in the elevator."

We forgave him, of course, but I did demand he use some of his hoarded allowance to buy a watch, so he could be back at a specified time and place. Unless, of course, he got stuck in the elevator again.

PUBLIC LAW 94-142

After we moved from Hot Springs, the words of the psychiatrist at the Seattle Children's Hospital came back to haunt me; "Regardless of circumstances, never let the school administrators put this child in special ed classes."

The first year in Fargo, North Dakota, Joel's school was a one-story building, so I didn't have to fuss. The following year meant junior high, a three-story building with no elevator. All of Joel's classes were on the second floor, except for a history class on the third. I could deal with the second floor by simply carrying him upstairs, setting him on a bench, going back for the wheelchair, carting it up, and plopping Joel in it, ready to go.

Because I worked mornings at a New York Life insurance office in downtown Fargo, to go back to school at a certain time every day to carry Joel to and from the third floor not only seemed ridiculous, it was impossible. So I asked the principal if the history class could be moved to the second floor.

"The special education classes are all on first floor. Joel can attend those classes," he replied to my request, completely ignoring "Public Law 94-142, Education of all Handicapped Children."

School board members and congressmen failed to answer my phone calls, so we did then what we should have done first, we visited the school superintendent, who lived in our neighborhood. He overruled the principal, and that weekend the maintenance men and the teacher moved the history class to the second floor. The teacher seemed glad to do this for Joel.

Not all teachers were compliant. When we moved to Bryan, Texas and enrolled Joel at Stephen F. Austin Junior High, all Joel's classes, except English, were on the first floor. The English teacher dug in her heels. "All my equipment is on the second floor," she said.

I appealed to the powers that be, and they gave orders to the English teacher. "For that class you teach downstairs."

She ignored the instructions. Joel sat downstairs alone. What would have happened to him had there been a fire, or some other disaster? Each time I complained, the teacher would have one class with Joel; then the next would be back upstairs.

Finally I told Joel, "I can't go to school and monitor this. When she leaves you downstairs alone, you wheel yourself down to the office and tell them."

This was before he got the electric wheelchair, and it was a labor intensive chore, but he followed my instructions. The teacher grudgingly complied, at least most of the time. Joel did not have a good school year.

However, Stephen F. Austin school impressed both Joel and I in one respect. The first afternoon I picked him up from school, I no sooner got him settled in the front seat of the van and the wheelchair loaded in the back, when we saw four or five students come out of the school. They marched out to the flagpole, one of them untied the rope that held the flag up, and slowly lowered it. The others stood at attention until the flag came down, then they helped fold it up, handling it with reverence and making sure it didn't touch the ground. When the flag was folded, they walked sedately back into the school. After that first time, Joel and I sat and watched the ceremony every day. It nearly always brought tears to my eyes.

Bryan High was a newer school, also two stories, but it had

elevators. By this time Joel proudly piloted his electric wheelchair. I'd take him to school, unload him, and he'd buzz merrily on his way.

But a different problem popped up. When Joel enrolled at the high school, the school administrator told me in no uncertain terms that if Joel attended regular classes, not to even think about using the special ed bus. That privilege, he said, belonged only to special ed kids. I'd been transporting Joel for years, so it didn't bother me.

Then Jill wrapped the back of the van around a tree and we were without transportation for a couple weeks, as we only owned one vehicle. Joel's beloved but heavy electric wheelchair hung like an albatross around our necks. I asked again about the possibility of Joel taking the special ed bus on a temporary basis. No way.

We managed by leaving the electric wheelchair at school, plugged into an electric receptacle to charge the batteries. We used the small wheelchair to wheel Joel back and forth. Whenever possible, Kay picked him up in her little red Datsun.

Though I did not win every battle for Joel, for the most part his school experience went well. He loved school, the teachers, with one exception, liked having him in their classes, and many of them told me things, such as, "The students interact well with Joel, and it's good for all of them."

BUGS, AGAIN

Jill finished high school and went to Fargo, North Dakota to graduate with her class, as she had previously arranged. She found work, and Leonard and Ruby Ringdahl took her in as a boarder. Without her to discuss items of interest with Joel, the house quieted. Empty nest syndrome loomed. Sure enough, Kay's senior year passed quickly, and she excitedly made plans to join Reubin and Lovie Englishbee in Alaska.

Their leaving hit Joel hard. I tried to compensate by giving him extra attention, but I could never do enough to make up for his two sisters.

Bugs the cat missed them, maybe even more than Joel did. His eating problem worsened. We let him out of the bedroom so he could roam around the house, but even that didn't remedy matters. He went around quietly and with big eyes, looking as though he wondered what had gone wrong with his world. Even though I fed that orange and white feline small amounts often, he still threw up regularly, so along with a nearly empty nest and a quiet son, I spent time cleaning up cat messes.

Bugs questioned what was wrong with his world, and so did Joel and I. When were the girls coming back? Were they coming back? It didn't look like it. Kay wrote, saying she thought she'd fly into North Dakota when she finished in Alaska, and probably would stay there rather than coming home. Jill flitted from job to job, as the economy in North Dakota hit a low and good jobs were scarce, but she did not want to leave, so was toughing it out.

As I cleaned up the second cat mess in one frustrating morning, I ran out of patience.

"I can't do this any longer," I told Joel. "I'm going to call and get an appointment to have him put to sleep." Joel frowned at the news but didn't argue. He understood how unhappy the family pet was.

Even though the veterinarian would not let me hold Bugs the cat while he did the job, I refused to leave the room. I wanted to make sure he finished the job he opposed doing, and did not give the cat to someone else. The phone call to Jill was terrible, but I made the call immediately after the deed was done.

Many years had passed since the old man came to the clinic door and asked me to put his dog to sleep and to keep the cat. Our kids extended the life of the little, large-eyed, orange and white cat with love and care. His premature end brought tears to all.

Maybe, if I'd had the patience and a hard enough heart to watch the cat grieve, the end wouldn't have had to come so soon. The girls came home. Jill arrived first, tired of looking for what turned out to be miserable jobs. She went job hunting the day after she came home to Texas and was offered three jobs, gratefully taking a pharmacy tech job at Eckerd's Drug. She worked there and at Winn Dixie a good share of the time she went to Texas A&M University.

True to her word, Kay flew from Alaska to Fargo, and like Jill, stayed with our friends, Leonard and Ruby Ringdahl. She applied for two jobs, didn't get either of them, and ran out of gumption quicker than her sister had. Knowing that Fred, Joel and I were visiting in Minnesota, she called us.

"Will you come and pick me up?"

Kay immediately went job hunting the day after we drove into the driveway in Texas. Luby's Cafeteria advertised for a cashier and Kay went to see the personnel manager there.

"I could give you this job, Kay," the lady told her. "But you can do much better than be a cashier here. I suggest you try."

The next job Kay applied for was at Ardan's–a department store of sorts. I don't think they had clothes, but maybe so. What I remember are the shelves full of china and knick-knacks. They gave her a job, a job which she enjoyed.

Our house livened up, with me even posting schedules on the fridge to keep track of who was coming home when.

JOEL'S LAST DAYS

Less than a month before Joel died, I took him to the MDA Clinic at Scott and White Medical Center, a routine visit. I realized he did not feel well that day, as while waiting for the doctor he asked to be taken out of his wheelchair so he could lie on the sofa in the waiting room. However, when the doctor examined him, between Joel's upbeat personality and the way he compensated for his lack of muscle strength, he fooled the doctor into thinking he was not terminal. After Joel died, this doctor called and apologized to us.

"I should have told you what to expect," he told us. "I would have advised keeping him at home to live his last days."

That sounds good in theory, but often the mucous in Joel's lungs made it nearly impossible for him to breathe. There was only one time that he lost consciousness before we brought him to the ER. During all other episodes, he stayed conscious and fought for breath, a terrible way to die.

The last three weeks of Joel's life he spent in St. Joseph's Hospital in Bryan, with a trachea tube inserted and on a respirator. I hated that trachea tube. Joel and I had always chattered together, and now he couldn't talk to me. During the day, I stayed with him, reading to him and combing his hair, which seemed to soothe him. At night his father would take his books and sit by Joel's bedside, sleeping some and studying some.

Kay and Jill came to the hospital many times, a hard thing for them. One evening Jill sneaked Joel's teddy bear hamster into his room. I saw a nurse peek in and see the little rodent scampering around on the bed, but she turned her back and got busy with something else.

***

Our family doctor came in one afternoon when I was with Joel. He sat on the edge of the bed and talked to him for a few minutes then asked, "Joel, if you go unconscious, do you want to be resuscitated?"

He shook his head, "No," emphatically.

We thought that settled the question, but it didn't happen that way. Fred was at the hospital when Joel stopped breathing. The code went out and Fred said the whole room filled with medical personnel. They brought life back, but not consciousness. Soon our son quit breathing again. He was gone. It was April 7, 1982.

A nurse called me and told me to come. This was when I made a huge mistake. I went into the girls' bedroom and told them, but didn't ask them whether or not they wanted to go with me—I just rushed and left. Fred stood outside the hospital sobbing.

The two of us went into the hospital room where Joel lay. I stood and looked at him for a while, "beeped" him on the nose and said, "I love you Jo lo," saying the name like Sue had done, and we copied often. She never could say "Joel" properly.

On the way home we saw Jill walking toward the hospital, crying. Immediately I realized my mistake. Why didn't I take the girls with me? Both Jennie and my folks were at the house, and I could have anticipated trouble. Years later, Jill told me my mother had said to her before she left the house, "Well, maybe you'll be happy now." What a cruel thing to say.

The funeral director insisted on a visitation the evening

before the funeral, but when I balked, he said our attendance wasn't necessary. Many people came to the visitation, including Joel's teachers, and we probably should have been there. It just seemed like too much for all of us, for the girls especially.

Jill and Kay asked young men of their acquaintance to sing: Stan Bone, Justin Bryan, John Egger, Mark Roberts and Steve Stack. We chose the hymn, "Oh for the Peace of a Perfect Trust" as it seemed appropriate for his life. The funeral is a blur. I remember sitting there holding hands with our daughters, Fred by our side, and I remember Dale Spencer spoke about David losing his son by Bathsheba.

Some of our friends likely thought us rude and heathenish when, first, we didn't go to the visitation, and second, we didn't have a lunch after the funeral. We simply went home: our family, Grandma Jennie, and my mom and dad. Fred's brother, Jim, and his wife, Mabel, came a few days later. Coming later was at Fred's request, as he wanted to see them after the funeral was over. People cope, some in one way and some in another. You manage to do the necessary things, even though it seems as though you're moving through slush. Nothing seems real.

***

The art teacher at Bryan High sent us a card and a note. Her classroom was located right where I came in and out of the school, bringing Joel in the morning, coming at noon to help with his bathroom duties and lunch, and picking him up at night. The note said:

"You were such an inspiration to me each morning as you and Joel arrived at school there by my door to start the day. There was so much love in your caring for him and he was such a positive fellow with a real place in life he'd made for himself. My heart goes out to you now for I know what an emptiness will be there."

This note from a person I never even met, just smiled and waved at when I'd see her through her open door, meant much to me and was one of only a few I have saved through the years.

***

After Fred finished his master's degree program, we would be moving to the Washington, D.C. area. To bury Joel in Texas seemed to me like scattering kids in our wake across the country, as Sue was interred in Lonepine Cemetery in Montana. Flying Joel's body to Montana for burial, we found out, was reasonable in price, so we decided on this course of action.

Fred was behind in his studies because of the three weeks he spent nights in the hospital with Joel. His orals loomed. I didn't want to leave Fred at this time. It seemed reasonable to just have Joel buried quietly without us in attendance and go to Montana later to visit his grave.

Jolene Jacobson, one of the rancher's wives, called. "You must have a service," she said. "Please contact your church people and arrange it."

We did. Later we found out they had also chosen, "Oh for the Peace of a Perfect Trust" to sing at the graveside. When writing this, I counted the names in the book from the graveside service, and was reminded that 149 people signed the book. This included every one of Joel's former grade school classmates.

***

I can write about my feelings, about the chasm left when he died, the funeral over and life back to as normal as it could get. I can write about how I didn't know what to do with my time. I can write about the tears that came when reading cards and writing thank you notes. I can even write about a feeling of relief, the same kind of relief I felt when we found out Joel's problem was muscular dystrophy. The worst that could happen was over. But I can't write much about Fred's feelings.

Much later, Fred told me about playing ball with Jill, Kay and Joel. This was back when Joel still walked. Fred demonstrated to the girls the proper stance to take to throw a ball.

When Joel's turn came, he took the stance naturally, and his ball throwing form was perfect. However, the ball landed about five feet in front of him. He simply did not have the strength necessary to throw a ball. It hit his father with force that, even if his son had great ability, the boy would never be able to do anything requiring even a minimal amount of strength. Fred couldn't stay out there with the kids, and he never tried to teach Joel sports again.

***

Things Joel taught us:

Accept help with a smile and a "thanks."
Trust. No one's going to drop you.
Be cheerful. It makes everyone feel better.
Laugh at every opportunity. Bad jokes are better than none.
Can't get into mischief by yourself? Find someone to help.

IS THIS WHAT WE WANT TO REMEMBER?

Pat Managhan headed the list of who we wanted to visit when Fred and I traveled back to Hot Springs in 2009. She came out to meet us when we drove into her neat yard, located on the corner where Highway 28 junctions with the road to town. When our conversation slowed down, Pat went into the other room and came out carrying a leather-tooled book.

"The Stellmon family and ours were very close when the kids were growing up. Our daughters felt like Larry Stellmon was a brother," she said, handing us the book. "After Larry joined the air force, he sent this to me. It shocked me, but I was so pleased. He wrote many memories of the fun we all had together. And he did the leather work himself," she said, pride evident in her voice. She chuckled. "Once in a while Larry would call me, tell me he'd flown over and waved, but he guessed I didn't see him."

Larry Stellmon was probably the closest thing to a celebrity that Hot Springs ever produced. He not only joined the air force, but became a Lieutenant Colonel and flew for the Thunderbirds.

I called Pat in October, 2013, before I finished the memoir. She is now 92 years of age, still lives by herself in her little home, and the day I called was stacking wood ready for the fireplace.

"There's a rumor going about town," she told me. "They say

the Good Lord doesn't want me and the devil is afraid of me." She paused. "I've had a heck of a good life."

After admiring the book Larry Stellmon had made for her, we all went to a café for lunch. Pat, even with the years working against her, walked up the steps with agility and confidence.

As we exited the café, a diesel pickup pulling a cattle trailer roared up and stopped across the parking lot. Two men jumped out and squinted into the sunlight.

"Hey, it's Doc," one yelled, and both strode over to greet us, with much laughter and slapping of backs. We stood in the spring sunshine and listened to the once-young men grown middle-aged, since our move from Montana 32 years before.

"Remember, Doc," said Steve with a smile, his blue eyes bright with memory. "Remember that ramp in our old barn? Once we called you to pull a calf, and there you stood with your back to that ramp, pulling a reluctant calf out of its ma's backside.

You put all your muscle into the job, strained like mad, and when that thing came out with a 'whoosh,' you collapsed on your butt, dropped the calf and 'whooshed' backward right down that ramp and into the manure. What a sight! We laughed so hard we thought we'd bust."

Fred stood there with a half-smile on his face. "Yeah, I should have billed you extra for the entertainment."

"I remember the rabies vaccination clinic I helped Doc with," added Mike, pushing his hat back. "A woman came in with a cat in a box. No top on the box, the cat just sat there like a statue. Until Doc reached for it, that is." Mike slapped his thigh and guffawed. "When Doc reached for that cat, the thing jumped straight in the air and landed, all claws out, on the lady's head. She screamed, the cat leaped down and disappeared. Had a heck of a time catching it."

He looked at me, then Steve. "You should have seen Doc's face. Looked like a bull acts when the back end of the chute clangs shut—surprised, worried, and mad all at the same time."

"That did take the cake," Fred retorted. "I had made a special point to tell everyone to put their cat in a carrier, knowing what a cat's reaction to the bedlam of people and dogs at the clinic would be. That one just sat like a bomb set to explode." He turned to Mike. "You remember the reason for the rabies clinic?"

"Vaguely. A woman caught rabies somehow."

"Right. A woman saw her cat playing with a half dead bat. Later the cat bit her. She told me her husband had to pry its jaws open it hung on so tight. We euthanized the cat and sent the head to the Veterinary Diagnostic Laboratory to test for rabies.

"Got a negative report, the preliminary one, but ten days later the mice injected with the cat's brain tissue started dying. Rabies. That shook everyone loose. In the race between the virus and the treatment, the virus had a two week head start."

"Yeah," Steve said. "They couldn't get the vaccine or whatever it's called, right?"

"Rabies immunoglobulin. She had to have the treatment before the virus got to her brain, and no one in Montana could supply it. Lots of red tape was cut before the U.S. Department of Public Health and the Centers for Disease Control delivered the globulin to Dr. Campbell. A few days sometimes seem like an eternity. I know they did to us, and I can only imagine how the woman felt."

"She did make it, didn't she?" asked Steve.

"Yep, the bureaucrats came through, and the globulin saved the woman's life."

Mike's brow furrowed. "Skunks came into the picture. Didn't they think skunks carried rabies? Is that why I trapped skunks?"

"Well, everyone knew our bats carried rabies and that east of the Continental Divide skunks did too. The public health officials wanted to make sure skunk rabies hadn't traveled here to Western Montana. That's why they sent one of the so-called expert government trappers to the area to trap skunks."

Fred looked at Mike and laughed. "It's a good thing his livelihood didn't depend on trapping skunks. He caught one skunk. In desperation, they called me and asked if I knew anyone who could trap, and I gave them your number, Mike. You proved to be a excellent skunk trapper. We all know what you smelled like." He chuckled. "Your Mom probably rejoiced when you finished the job. How many skunks did you trap?"

"Twenty-one, or thereabouts. Then they called and said, 'Enough already. Don't send any more skunk heads.' They paid well. Worth the stink."

I stood in the gravel parking lot wishing for a tape recorder and wondered; do they remember any brilliant diagnoses, any excellent treatment, any good service? Their affection, their joy at seeing their old vet, answered that question. They all remembered the good. But the bad makes a better story.

***

After the conversation with Mike and Steve outside the café, I started remembering some moments those two men didn't know about.

On a quiet afternoon, as Fred and I sat at the desk and waded through drug company invoices, a woman rushed through the door and dumped a dead cat on the exam table.

"I want this cat checked for rabies. He bit my baby."

She stood by the cat, which lay grotesquely sprawled on the table, but she didn't look at it. Neither did she look directly at either Fred or me. Her gaze circled the room while her hands rubbed her jeans.

"Sure. We can do that." Fred jumped up and walked to the exam table. "It hasn't been dead long, it's still pliant and warm.

We'll send the head into the lab right away."

"Is the baby okay?" I asked.

"My husband's taking her to the doctor."

Fred turned the cat over, a puzzled look on his face. "How did you kill the cat?"

The woman shuffled her feet and didn't answer. A question mark seemed glued in the air, and no one said anything. Then she blurted out, "I didn't want to tell you, you'll think I'm some kind of a monster." She swiped at her hair. "I came in the room when the baby cried out and saw him biting her. I killed him."

"I still don't see how you did it. There aren't any wounds on the body." He paused, then added, "Not that it matters."

Tears came into the mother's eyes. "We had the cat four years and loved him. He never did anything like this before." Looking down at the floor she mumbled, "I took him and just pulled. Stretched him until he quit struggling. Until he quit breathing. Until his heart quit."

Fred and I both involuntarily glanced at the woman's bare arms, which bore no visible scratches. We marvel yet at this mother who killed her pet cat with bare hands to protect her baby. Happily, the cat turned out to be rabies free.

***

My mind went back to another incident. Home from a shopping trip to Missoula, my little girls, arms full of packages, reached the house before I even slammed the car door shut. Kay opened the front door and all three nearly fell inside. "Hey, Patti," yelled Jill. "Come, see what we bought in Missoula!" The blonde teenager walked slowly into the kitchen, where packages littered the table. Patti's normally well-combed ponytail hung lower than usual, and hair dangled in her harried-looking eyes. She pulled out a chair and flopped into it.

The girls excitedly pulled shorts, skirts, socks out, expecting

Patti's compliments and comments. "That's nice Kay," she said, when shown a blue dress. "Oh, blue socks to match." Her lackluster voice alerted the girls.

"What's wrong, Patti?" Kay asked. "You sick?"

"No. Just tired." She looked at me. "How in the world do you do it, Georgia? You left me with the baby, the phone, the dogs, the people stopping in for vaccine. But you normally take care of the three girls plus the baby, the phone, the dogs, the clients, the drug reps, the bookwork. You even help with treatment and surgery, and whoever knows what else."

"You normally handle it well, Patti. What happened today?" I smiled at her woeful face.

"I just finished changing the baby when the phone rang. I put him into his crib and answered the kitchen phone. As I talked on the phone, a pickup drove up. I hung up and, of course, forgot to write down the message." Making a wry face, she continued. "As I passed the patio door, I saw three dogs outside hightailing it to freedom." She smiled at me guiltily, "I must not've latched the dog run securely when I fed them."

Interested in her tale, I pulled out a chair and sat down. "So what did you do first?"

She pushed hair out of her eyes. "I went to the clinic, greeted Percy Cottet, and answered the phone out there. The message is on the desk—a downer cow—so I radioed Doc to tell him. Percy wanted vaccine, and I started figuring out dosages. Then the dogs ran past the clinic door. Percy saw them and asked, 'What's with the dogs, Patti?' I told him my sad story about the three escaped dogs, which I needed to corral—if they weren't out of the county by the time I got out there. 'Okay,' he said. 'Leave the vaccine and let's go out and see if we can coax those dogs in.'"

"That sounds like Percy."

"We opened the door and the dogs scattered in three different directions. I could see myself telling Doc three boarders flew the coop, figured we'd never get them in. But, surprisingly, two of them came when I called. Percy grabbed one, and I grabbed the other. The white shaggy one stayed just out of our reach, but we finally lured him in with a doggie treat. I made sure I latched the door that time."

Sue put her arms on Patti's lap and looked up at her face, listening.

"Before I finished getting Percy's order put up, another rancher drove up. And the phone rang again. That's the way it went all afternoon. I did manage to diaper and feed Joel in between, but I didn't have much time to play with him. He's sleeping again now. I was *so* glad to see your car drive up." She picked Sue up. "Now girls, I want to see what else you have in those packages."

The phone rang. Gravel crunched in the drive. I grinned. "My turn, Patti." After I took care of the phone and the client, I came back in and told Patti the following story.

"As you know, Patti, many times in the spring we're too busy to do elective surgery on dogs and cats, so we put up temporary stalls for scouring calves in the dog runs. Fred sets up IV's and during the day I keep the IV bottles full and stuff boluses down the calves' throats. The room is smelly in spite of my frequent ministrations with the water hose.

Patti nodded. "Stinks awful, I know."

"One morning I hosed the place down, then realized I'd better get to the bathroom before I peed in my pants. I practically ran to the bathroom off the kitchen, unzipping my jeans as I went. I made it in time. Just. Before I finished, I heard the phone. I figured I'd answer it in the kitchen." I paused, "We need one of those newfangled telephone answering machines around here. This phone is driving us all nuts.

"The kitchen door always seems to be open, and you can see into the kitchen from the clinic, another thing we plan to change. Anyway, about the time I finished my toilet job and heard the phone ringing, a pickup door slammed. I rushed past the open kitchen door pulling up my jeans. 'Gee. I can't even take a leak in this place,' I complained aloud."

Patti almost smiled; she'd heard me talk to myself.

"I answered the phone, came through the kitchen door into the clinic and saw Arvid Kopp. Or I saw the back of Arvid Kopp. A terrible thought seized me. Just how quickly did he get into the clinic? Did he see me pulling up my jeans? Did he hear my loud comment about taking a leak? As soon as I thought it, I knew. I stood there wanting to quietly disappear while Arvid ostensibly studied a horse picture. His shoulders shook. Yes. He had seen me. Yes. He had heard me. 'Hello, Arvid,' I said. My face felt hot. Really hot.

Having gotten his laughter under control, Arvid turned around. For the second time he saw pink cheeks. No one ever said anything to me, but you know Arvid Kopp, Patti. He probably got lots of laughs relating that one."

Patti, her tale of woe forgotten, went cheerfully out the door.

Dr. Robert M. Miller cartoon

***

Many of my bad moments came because I didn't have enough authority to make the ranchers listen to instructions. Orville Bjorge brought a beautiful little Hereford heifer calf into the clinic one February, which is when the calving season began. I babied that scouring calf for three days, nursing it back to health. Fred finally told me to call Orville to come fetch his calf. Knowing Orville, Fred was emphatic, "Do *not* let him throw her in the back of his pickup," Fred said. "She'll get chilled and get the scours again."

Fred left. Orville came. He backed his pickup to the door. "Orville," I said, as forcefully as I could, "Fred left strict instructions not to put that calf in the back of your pickup or it'll get sick again. He said to put it in the cab and keep it warm."

Orville looked at me like I had two heads. "That calf ain't going in the cab. It'll crap all over."

Forgetting forcefulness, I desperately implored him. "It'll get sick again. It's doing great now." Orville paid no attention to me.

"There's straw back there. It'll be fine," he said, threw the calf in the back and got in the pickup. The calf's large brown eyes looked at me, her foster mother so to speak, as he revved the motor and took off.

Two days later Orville called. "Just as I thought," he told me. "That calf died. Could just as well've saved the money and let her die in the first place."

My fingers tightened on the receiver, like they were around Orville's neck. I couldn't say, "I told you to put her in the cab," even though it was exactly what I wanted to say. The calf died because I did not have the authority, the clout, that Fred exhibited.

***

Another client, a successful logger and lumberman with money enough to build up a herd of cattle, brought a dying cow in from the west end of the county. In the 1970's, cattlemen got the notion to import exotic breeds into the U.S. from Europe, breeds such as Charolais, Simmental, Limousin and Aquitaine Blond.

A cow can only throw one calf a year. In contrast, through artificial insemination, semen from only one bull can impregnate hundreds of cows. This fact made females more valuable than males. The client wanted to have a corner on Aquitaine Blond females, a less popular exotic breed, by owning a majority of the half Aquitaine Blond cows in the U.S.

His cow, bred to an Aquitaine Blond bull, was about eight months pregnant and had a blocked digestive tract. Fred and the rancher talked it over and decided to not risk doing surgery on the cow and losing the calf. Fred induced her into labor, and she produced a premature calf.

"The gods of reproduction gave us a heifer," were the grateful words from the client.

We fixed a cozy corner in the clinic for her, away from any scouring calves. My boss gave me strict instructions: disinfect your boots, wash carefully before going in to care for it, and most important, feed it a small amount often.

"This is one expensive calf," my husband told me. "If she grows up and has a heifer, that heifer will be 7/8 Aquitaine and will be registered as a purebred. We have to take good care of this one."

I followed instructions to the letter. To overload a normal

young calf gives it digestive problems. This delicate, premature calf with its sensitive digestive tract required small, frequent feedings.

The heifer gradually gained strength and the rancher came to pick her up. Tall, good-looking, he had the particular brand of self-confidence that comes with money. Unlike so many, he actually seemed to listen as I gave him instructions.

"You must feed her only a small amount." I showed him how much, and then said, "Feed her every two hours. Gradually increase the amount, but if you feed her too much at a time she'll die." I looked him in the eye. "It's important." He promised to obey me, loaded up his calf in the cab of his truck, like I told him, and left.

Several days later he called. "The calf died."

Thunderstruck, I asked, "Were you careful not to feed her too much at a time?"

He hesitated, then confessed. "She seemed very healthy. After feeding her, she acted so hungry I fed her again. She died in just a few hours!"

It was another instance of me just not having the authority I needed to get the job done properly.

***

Not being aggressive enough with the clients wasn't always the problem. One spring day Fred admitted a large, Hereford cross critter into the clinic. The calf was dehydrated because of scours. As it was too big to fit into our temporary scouring calf stalls, Fred herded it into a dog run, where it collapsed on the floor. He treated it, and before he left on ranch calls, gave me instructions to put a tube down the calf's throat and pour milk into it.

"Can I do that? He's a big one."

"It should be done before I get back. You've done it before.

211

You'll do fine."

I looked at the huge calf and felt the wrinkle between my eyes deepen. If I put the tube down wrong and it ended up in the trachea, I would drown the poor thing.

The day went fast, much faster than usual. Afternoon came. Would Fred finish quicker than he thought and come home? No such luck. Finally I could put it off no longer, so gathered the stuff I needed. Hoisting the heavy calf to an upright position, I held him as straight as I could between my knees, and slid the tube down his throat. Sweat gathered on my forehead like dew on a blade of grass, and it wasn't because it was warm.

The tube down, I blew into it and smelled the air coming out. I knew it should smell sour like ingesta. Did it smell right? I sniffed again. Surely there must be a better way than this, I thought, as I blew and sniffed. Should I take it out and try again? It smelled funny, but maybe not funny enough. Finally, I told myself, it must be down the esophagus and into the stomach, the trachea wouldn't smell like that. After hesitating a long moment, I slowly poured milk into the tube. Done, I pulled the tube out and laid the calf's head down, relief making me lean against the wall.

It was a temporary relief. Within moments the calf stiffened and died. I couldn't believe it. I'd been so careful. But the evidence shouted at me—I had drowned the calf by running a half gallon of milk into his lungs. Calling to tell a good client I killed his calf was my lowest point in the years I served as Fred's veterinary technician.

Our marriage contract still in effect, and not able to afford better help, Fred didn't, or couldn't, fire me. I continued to follow him around on his morning clinic rounds, a clipboard and pencil in hand, as I wrote down instructions for the day.

***

Orville Branson brought in a purebred polled Hereford heifer destined for shipment to South Africa. Among many other things, the authorities required a TB test. The Montana Veterinary Exam Board's semi-annual board meeting came up at the same time the TB test had to be read. Fred, a member of the Board, gave me instructions and drove merrily away for a few days.

How often I herded that heifer into the chute and checked her test site, I don't remember. I do remember the difficulty. An extremely skittish animal, even when I slowly and quietly mucked out her stall, she'd cower in the corner.

To get her out of the stall and into the chute made me nearly as anxiety-ridden as the heifer. No matter how quiet, how careful I tried to be, she'd bolt out of the stall, skate over the roughened concrete floor, eyes wild, turn the corner on two legs, and skid into the chute. I was sure she'd do the splits and break a leg.

Normally I rather liked it when the boss was away for a few days. Things quieted down and I could do a project or two of my own. This time I greeted Fred's arrival home with fervor. Survival with no broken bones meant success.

***

Success was elusive when it came to Don Perrin's statements. Tall, dark and handsome, likely in his forties, quiet, with a slight stutter, Don blushed easily. He stopped one day shortly after the first of the month.

"Georgia, I-I-I think you've made-made, a mis-mis-take on my bill."

I smiled at him. "That's certainly possible. What do you have there?" He clutched his monthly statement and slips from the different ranch calls. We soon located the mistake, mine, of course, and settled up. He escaped gratefully, more embarrassed about my mistake than I was.

However, the next month Don appeared at the office again, Stetson in one hand, that month's statement and slips in the other. His color high, his stutter more pronounced he said, "I - - I think there's a mis - - mis - - take on my bill." He didn't say, "You idiot, you've done it again," like I deserved. Again we settled up, and he disappeared quickly and quietly.

The next month Don slunk in just when Fred popped out of the pharmacy and into the office. "Hello Don. What can I do for you?" he asked.

Poor Don. Stammering and stuttering he showed Fred another billing mistake. I sat at the desk listening and could hardly believe it. Surely not again? I thought I'd checked that statement at least twice. Don showed the statement to Fred who first nodded, then grinned.

"You're right, Don. The problem is my wife. I suspect she makes these mistakes deliberately. She likes for you to come in."

I blushed even more furiously than Don, and vowed then and there to never, ever send a statement to Don without Fred scrutinizing it carefully. I couldn't bear to make the poor man go through that again.

In James Herriot's book *All Creatures Great and Small*, Seigfried Farnon says to his new veterinary assistant, James. "It's a funny profession, ours, you know. It offers unparalleled opportunities for making a chump of yourself."

***

Our children started life in Montana, competing for attention with sick animals, the telephone, and a constant parade of big-hatted, dirty-booted ranchers striding through the clinic door. Few children have the opportunities our kids experienced; seeing the mess and smelling the often sickening odors involved in birth, in sickness, and in death.

The physical odors and messes of life are one thing, but I often wonder about other influences on our family life, such as our moves from Montana to North Dakota and then to Texas. And what would our family be like had Sue and Joel lived? What kind of persons would they have become, and how would their lives have affected the rest of us?

Little twists of fate can change a personality, a way of looking at life, and can change the way a person treats others. We'll never know what might have been just as we don't know what the rest of life holds. Maybe that's why us humans cling to life even when times are tough–we simply want to stick around to know the rest of the story.

Georgia Alderink and her husband, Fred, retired to Arkansas where, in spite of their advancing years, in spite of the heat, and even in spite of the ticks and chiggers, they enjoy the Ozark hiking trails. When they do stay inside, Georgia sits at her computer putting words together. After having published two children's books, magazine articles, and stories in three anthologies, she ran out of creative ideas and turned to memoir.

38331871R00126

Made in the USA
Lexington, KY
03 January 2015